KEIR
HARDIE

Copyright © 2010 Bob Holman
This edition copyright © 2010 Lion Hudson

A Lion Book
an imprint of
Lion Hudson plc
Wilkinson House, Jordan Hill Road,
Oxford OX2 8DR, England
www.lionhudson.com
ISBN 978 0 7459 5354 0

Distributed by:
UK: Marston Book Services, PO Box 269, Abingdon, Oxon, OX14 4YN
USA: Trafalgar Square Publishing, 814 N. Franklin Street, Chicago, IL 60610
USA Christian Market: Kregel Publications, PO Box 2607, Grand Rapids, MI 49501

First edition 2010
10 9 8 7 6 5 4 3 2 1 0

Typeset in 11.5/14 Minion Pro

BOB HOLMAN

KEIR HARDIE

LABOUR'S GREATEST HERO?

LION

To our family

CONTENTS

PREFACE

I had wanted to write about Keir Hardie ever since I first came to live in his part of Scotland – Lanarkshire, Ayrshire and Glasgow – in the 1970s. But in the business of retirement, including looking after our two grandsons, I was reluctant to leave too much on my wife's shoulders. Her response was short and sharp, as becomes a Scot, "You must do Hardie." So thanks, Annette. Our son, David, and daughter, Ruth, along with our son-in-law, Bruce, and our beloved grandsons, Lucas and Nathan, have all groaned when I announced my latest bit of Hardie trivia such as, "Did you know that Hardie was a keen cricket player?" But it was a supportive groan.

From 2008 I was making the seventy-mile drive to Cumnock in Ayrshire where Hardie lived for much of his life. Here the Baird Institute possesses a number of documents relating to him, along with certain items which had once been in his office, lodged in what was known as the Hardie Room. I wish to thank staff members of the East Ayrshire Council, Linda Fairlie and Gibson Kyte, for their cheerful helpfulness.

My publishing contacts with Lion Publishing go back thirty years. Now as Lion Hudson plc, I received immediate encouragement from Kate Kirkpatrick. Editors tend to dislike too many references but I have listed a considerable number. To shorten them, I have not given specific references for every quotation from Hardie (and from his daughter Nan) for speeches and articles. At the end of the book, I do list the relevant journals in which his talks and writings appeared.

Introduction

Lord Overtoun was a wealthy Victorian factory-owner in Glasgow and a prominent supporter of the Liberal Party. He was also a well-known Christian noted for his gifts to charities, his financial support to foreign missions, his provision of a £1,000 salary to a local evangelist, and his backing for campaigns to keep the Sabbath holy.

In 1899 Keir Hardie, also a Christian but one of very limited financial means, launched a fierce attack on Overtoun. In a widely read pamphlet, he revealed how Overtoun treated his workers in his chemical works at Rutherglen in Glasgow. They were made to toil for twelve hours a day with no food breaks, seven days a week. Deadly fumes were likely to poison their lungs. He accused Overtoun of being a hypocrite who even docked the wages of men who did not work on Sundays. The Glasgow clergy, almost to a man, rose to defend Overtoun and condemned Hardie as an atheist. Hardie soon responded.

More will be written of the Overtoun affair in a later chapter. Here it is sufficient to say that, throughout his life, Hardie both proclaimed Christianity and attacked those Christians and churches who tolerated huge poverty, sufferings, and inequalities.

Who was this Keir Hardie? In Glasgow, I asked some school children if they knew about Robert Burns. All did, always attended a Burns Night at school, and had been to visit his birthplace and homes in Ayrshire. None had heard of Keir Hardie, let alone visited the place where he lived for over thirty years, also in Ayrshire. In 2009 Scotland was agog with celebrations to mark 250 years since the birth of Burns. Three years previously, in 2006, the 150th birthday of Keir Hardie was hardly noticed.

Yet Hardie was one of the founders of the Labour Party and its first leader in the House of Commons. He was immensely popular among many working-class supporters yet hounded by the press. Initially as an MP he stood completely alone. Many MPs in other parties – and not a few in his own – disliked him.

In some ways, he is still an enigma. He wrote no autobiography, penned just a handful of pages in a diary, kept hardly any of the thousands of letters he must have received. On the other hand, he wrote numerous articles in papers and magazines.

Hardie had several early biographers. More recent academic writers tend to dismiss them as hagiographers who failed to see his limitations. Certainly, for instance, William Stewart, in *J. Keir Hardie*, a book published six years after Hardie's death, makes no mention of his illegitimacy. David Lowe in his *From Pit to Parliament* in 1923 avoids the question of Hardie's close relationship with Sylvia Pankhurst, as does Emrys Hughes, Hardie's son-in-law, in *Keir Hardie*, published in 1956. Yet two points must be made. First, they were not silent on some of his limitations, particularly his growling temper and his failures, as a leader in the Commons. Second, they all knew Hardie and his family. Thus David Lowe wrote, "I knew Keir Hardie well – perhaps no-one knew him better. I knew his father and his mother, his sisters and his brothers; worked, travelled, slept, discussed, smoked and laughed with him, and yet I always retained an intact liberty to differ with him."[1] William Stewart knew Hardie and, after his death, interviewed his wife Lillie Hardie, his brothers, several miners who knew him in his early years, and supporters who campaigned with him in West Ham and Merthyr. These are the writers who "felt" the real Hardie.

The academic Hardie specialists include Iain McLean in *Keir Hardie* (1975), Kenneth Morgan in his widely read *Keir Hardie. Radical and Socialist* (1975), and Fred Reid in *Keir Hardie. The Making of a Socialist* (1978). They differ between themselves on the factors which shaped Hardie's behaviour, the extent to which Hardie was a socialist, when he became a socialist, and what his achievements were. But all agree he was a major political figure.

Particular mention must be made of Caroline Benn's exhaustive – and sometimes exhausting – *Keir Hardie* (1997). She brilliantly draws together the historical material relevant to Hardie and produces a sympathetic but not uncritical biography. I have drawn upon her considerably. She observes that many biographers have felt "ill at ease" with his religion.[2] Although not a Christian herself, she does give serious attention to his religion and sees it as one of his phases which developed from "temperance campaigning to evangelical Christianity to 'new union' militancy; from free speech campaigns to women's suffrage and finally to war resistance".[3] A major theme of my book will be to place more importance on his religious faith than most previous biographers. I will develop it not as a passing enthusiasm when he was a church leader in his twenties but as one of the main factors in his personal and political life until the end.

Christian writers of late have published lives of several political Christians, including John Milton, William Wilberforce, Lord Shaftesbury, Jonathan Aitken, and Tony Blair. None has written about Keir Hardie. Fred Reid explains that apart from historians "practically nobody remembers him".[4] Perhaps this is partly because of the fact that the Labour Party is now so different from the one he helped to form. Kenneth Morgan, a historian with several distinguished studies of the Hardie period, concludes that he is now an "almost forgotten figure".[5]

On entering the town of Cumnock, where Hardie spent

the major part of his life, there is no sign to indicate that this great man had lived there. In a small way I hope to bring the forgotten leader back to the attention of today's readership.

Never a Child, 1856–78

Hardie's Scotland, the Scotland of the nineteenth century, experienced a huge growth in industry, commerce, trade, and financial institutions, with resultant large incomes for many citizens. Yet, as Professor T. C. Smout states in his seminal study, there were losers as well as winners. He wrote, "The age of great industrial triumphs was an age of appalling social deprivation. I am astounded by the tolerance… of unspeakable urban squalor, compounded by drink abuse, bad housing, low wages, long hours and sham education."[1] This too was Hardie's Scotland.

Over the century, partly as a result of improvements in machinery, the numbers of jobs in farming and textiles declined by half. Some would have obtained employment in the growing coal-mining industry but found themselves subject to fluctuating demand and no job security. Smout continues that miners, in particular, "generally had no option but to live in company houses which were among the most inadequate and disgusting of all Scotland's miserable housing stock".[2]

For instance in 1892 in Auchenraith there were 492 people who lived in 42 single-room and 41 two-room houses, who had no wash houses and shared twelve doorless privies, an open sewer, and two drinking fountains. It was no wonder that miners and their families were exposed to dreadful diseases above the ground while the men suffered coal-related illnesses and severe accidents below. Hardie was a miner.

The hard labour and long hours were not compensated by adequate incomes. In 1867, unskilled workers (30 per cent of the total) received on average £20 10s. a year while one earner in three hundred (and not always earners but those whom Hardie called the "idle rich" whose money was derived from rents, shares, and dividends) received an average of £3,952 a year. Nor was there any state unemployment pay or pension. Those who suffered unemployment, sickness, or old age had no recourse but grudging charity or the workhouse.

At least Hardie was born in a Britain which had passed the Reform Acts of 1832. In fact, for all their fame, their outcomes in terms of extending the vote were small. In Scotland, the number of men with votes rose to a mere 65,000. The Scottish Reform Act of 1868 made a larger impact, with the vote granted to ratepaying male householders and £10-a-year lodgers in towns and to small owners and tenants paying a middling rent in the countryside. The larger electorate also led to greater local party activity in selecting candidates, winning support, and getting voters to polling stations. The victory of the Tories in the general election of 1874 was partly attributed to their improved local organization.

Welcome as it was, the extended franchise made little difference to the kinds of people who became MPs or the nature of political parties. MPs – who were unpaid and required money for electoral expenses – continued to be drawn from the aristocracy, very wealthy businessmen, and members of the professions, particularly lawyers. The number of working-class MPs was minimal and the few who were elected were paid by and so were dependent upon a political party. The two main parties (apart from Irish MPs), the Liberals and the Tories, continued to dominate politics and to rule in their own interests. Scotland had long been in the hands of the Liberals, who were seen as more sympathetic toward working people. In his early life, Hardie favoured them.

A HARD CHILDHOOD

Hardie was born on 15 August 1856, in a one-room house in Legbrannock, near Holytown in Lanarkshire, some ten miles from Glasgow. His mother, Mary Paterson, was a farm servant who lived with her mother Agnes. At the age of twenty-six, she had become pregnant by a miner, William Aitken, against whom she successfully pursued a paternity suit. She called the baby James Keir.

Aitken took no interest and probably did not, as the sheriff court had ordered, pay Mary £1 10s. for lying-in expenses and £6 a year. Mary continued to work in the fields. Grandmother Agnes looked after the child. She was a story teller and singer and Keir Hardie (as he became known) later spoke fondly of her. He could play in the fields and he always had a streak which looked back upon rural Britain with affection.

In 1859 Mary married a ship's carpenter from Falkirk, David Hardie, in the Church of Scotland in Holytown on 21 August 1859. In time she was to have a further six sons and two daughters by him. David was a resolute and sensible man who always sought work and accepted Keir as his own son – except when he got drunk and called him "bastard". They moved to Glasgow to seek work found in a Govan shipyard. Nonetheless, the growing family made life a financial struggle.

Mary was always keen that Keir should be educated. She probably taught him the basics, for she could certainly read. It may be that he attended a school for a very short period. There are references to a clergyman who gave him lessons. The boy responded with enthusiasm and would pick up discarded newspapers as his lesson books.

The Education Act (1872) which established compulsory education for five- to thirteen-year-olds came just too late for Keir Hardie. He started work aged eight, which is probably what he meant when he later said, "I am of the unfortunate class who never knew what it was to be a child." Hamilton Fyfe cites Hardie as saying: "Under no circumstances, given freedom of choice, would I live that part of my life over again."[3] He was referring to his working childhood. From being a message boy in Glasgow he moved on to a printer's and then a brass-fitting shop. The latter did not last, as his parents discovered that he would go unpaid for a year as part of his apprenticeship. Next he was in Thompsons Shipyards, heating up rivets for men to hammer in. The work was carried out at a height and, when the boy next to him fell to his death, Mary immediately withdrew Keir from the place.

Matters got worse. David Hardie suffered an accident which meant he could not work. By the time he recovered, a recession and shipyard strike had started in 1866. The family were forced to sell their meagre possessions and moved to one room in Partick. Keir was the breadwinner, with 3s. 6d. a week from a high-class baker's with his job delivering bread and rolls. There followed an incident which engraved itself into Hardie's being. It is best to use his words written many years later.

My hours were from 7am to 7.30pm. I was the eldest of a family of three and the brother next to me was down with fever, from which he never recovered, though his life dragged on for two years thereafter. As most of the neighbourhood had children, they feared coming into the house because of the danger of contagion, and my mother, who was very near her confinement, was in delicate health.

It was the last week of the year. Father had been away for two or three days in search of work. Towards the end of the week, having been up most of the night, I got to the shop fifteen minutes' late and was told by the young lady in charge that if it occurred again I would be punished. I made no reply. I couldn't. I felt like crying. Next morning the same thing happened – I could tell why, but that is neither here nor there. It was a very wet morning, and I reached the shop drenched to the skin, barefooted and hungry. There had not been a crust of bread in the house that morning.

But this was payday, and I was filled with hope. "You are wanted upstairs by the master," said the girl behind the counter, and my heart almost stopped beating. Outside the dining room a servant bade me wait till "master had finished prayers" (he was much noted for his piety). At length the girl opened the door, and the sight of that room is fresh in my memory even as I write, nearly fifty years after. Round a great mahogany table sat the members of the family, with the father at the top. In front of him was a very wonderful looking coffee boiler, in the great glass bowl of which the coffee was bubbling. The table was loaded with dainties. My master looked at me over his glasses, and said, in quite a pleasant tone of voice – "Boy, this is the second morning you have been late, and my customers leave me if they are kept waiting for their hot breakfast rolls. I therefore dismiss you, and to make you more careful in the future, I have decided to fine you a week's wages. And now you may go!"

I wanted to speak and explain about my home, and I muttered out something to explain why I was late but the servant took me by the arm and led me downstairs. As I passed through the shop the girl in charge gave me a roll and said a kind word. I knew my mother was waiting for my wages. As the afternoon was drawing to a close I ventured home, and told her what had happened. It seemed to be the last blow. The roll was still under my vest but soaked with rain. That night the baby was born, and the sun rose on the 1st January, 1867, over a home in which there was neither fire nor food, though, fortunately, relief came before the day had reached its noon. But the memory of these early days abides with me, and makes me doubt the sincerity of those who make pretence in their prayers. For such things still abound in our midst.

The incident planted in Hardie a venomous scorn of hypocritical wealthy Christians. As an adult he became a Christian and his life was characterized by his love for Christianity and his dislike of many so-called Christians.

THE MINER

Later that year, David Hardie went back to sea, which was the only place he could obtain work, as a ship's carpenter. The family moved to the small mining village of Newarthill. On the very day his father left, ten-year-old Keir started work in the pits owned by the Monkland Iron Company for a shilling a day. He worked from 6 a.m. to 5.30 p.m. six days a week plus four hours on Sunday. This did not count his three-mile walk to and from the pit. In winter, he hardly ever saw the sun. William Stewart, in a biography written for the Independent Labour Party six years after Hardie's death, adds that at this time, although it may well have been later, "he began to attend Fraser's night school at Holytown… There was no light provided in the school and pupils had to bring their own candles."[4] Here he learned the rudiments of grammar and syntax.

His job was that of "a trapper", that is he operated the trap door that let air into the mine-shaft. Aged twelve, he was promoted to draw the pit ponies underground. Mining was dangerous enough. As many pit-owners cut costs by ignoring legal safety standards, which were rarely applied, it became increasingly threatening. Before long, Keir Hardie was involved in a pit accident. Again, it is best to write what he recorded after the event.

My pony was a little shaggy Highlander, appropriately named Donald – strong and obstinate, like the race among whom he had been reared. We were great friends and drank tea from the same tin flask, sip about... Donald and I were jogging along, when the voice of Rab Mair, the big, genial fireman, came reverberating out of the gloom, his little lamp shining like a star in the blackness: "Run into the dook and warn the men to come at once; the shank's closin." I did not stay on the order of my going. The shank closing! The shank is the shaft by which entrance and egress to the pit is obtained. It was the only outlet. Should it close in we were entombed, and what that might mean I did not care to think. In a very short time all the men were at the pit bottom, only to find that already they were too late. We were seventy fathoms from the daisies, and the weary rocks tired of hanging in mid-air seemed bent on settling down into some semblance of solidarity. For once in a way the drip of water could not be heard. The timber props were creaking and bursting all around us; while strong rocks were groaning and cracking and roaring as they were settling down. As man after man rushed to the bottom breathless and alarmed, they were met with the news that already the cage, by which men and material are taken to the surface, was "stuck in the shank". The sides of the shaft had so far come together that the cage had no longer a free passage and was held fast some fathoms above us. We were prisoners.

I can recall every detail of the scene. The men gathered in groups, each with his little lamp on his bonnet, their blackened, serious faces discussing what should be done. The roaring and crackling, as if of artillery, went on overhead and gloom began to settle on every countenance. Some of the more susceptible were crying, and I remember two by themselves who were praying and crossing themselves. Rab Mair remained cool and strong, and did his best to keep up the spirits of his fellow-prisoners. By and by I began to feel sleepy, and made my way to the stables whither Donald had already gone. By this time it was evident the worst of the crisis was over; the noise overhead was subsiding and the drip of the water was again to be heard. But the shaft was closed. We were prisoners indeed. After cleaning Donald down, I gave him a feed of corn, put some hay in his manger, and rolling myself in this, kissed him, as was our wont, and then went to sleep. A boy of twelve will sleep when there is nothing to do, even if he is cooped in a trap. How long I slept I have no means of knowing. It was Rab Mair's voice – swearing if the truth must be told – and some vigorous punches from his fist which brought me back to consciousness.

The engineman, on finding the cages stuck fast in the shaft, and hearing the signals from below, knew there was something wrong and raised the alarm. In a short time the news spread and soon the bulk of the people were at the pit, my mother among the rest. Volunteers were plentiful, and soon some brave fellows had been lowered by an improvised kettle into the shaft, where they soon discovered what was amiss. Cold chisels, picks and saws were requisitioned, and the imprisoned cages cut free and allowed to drop in pieces to the bottom after which the kettle – a bucket used by pit sinkers, and narrower than the cage – was used to bring the imprisoned men to the surface. But where was the trapper? Everyone had seen him in the bottom, and perhaps in the excitement of the moment no one would have missed him had there not been a mother there waiting for him. And so Rab Mair and two companions had to descend into the depths again and search. For a time their searching was in vain until Rab bethought him of Donald's crib and there sure enough I was, sound asleep. Rab pretended to be angry – but he wasn't. I think the reception on the top was the most trying part of the affair. At least, it was the only part where I cried.

The twelve-year-old had heard about pit accidents and now he had experienced one. Later he was to campaign strongly for effective legislation to be implemented to reduce their numbers. Trade unionism was not strong in this mine but he had witnessed the readiness of other miners to endanger themselves for the sake of colleagues. Not least, Keir Hardie never failed to identify people such as Rab Mair whose character and ability stood out.

The census of 1871 reveals that the family lived at 88 Durngaber Rows, Quarter Iron Works. It consisted of David Hardie (46), his wife Mary (38), James, that is Keir (14), Agnes (9), Alex (7), William (4) and David (2 months). Mary could not have envisaged in her wildest dreams that two of these boys (plus George, yet to be born) would become MPs.

When Keir was about seventeen, David Hardie, having returned home, found a job as a carpenter at the Quarter Iron Works. The family moved again and were housed in a colliers' row with no sanitation and no running water. The Franco-Prussian War lessened competition from coalfields abroad and wages rose. The Hardie youngsters had boots and a second set of clothes. Then the enterprising Mary opened a shop in her house which undercut prices in the Ironmaster's own store. David Hardie was ordered to shut it. Writers have sometimes overlooked that he too was a resolute and principled man: he refused and was sacked.

David and Mary had abandoned religion under the influence of the freethinker Charles Bradlaugh, whose writings they seemed to know, at least by report. But they had no objections to lessons being given to Keir by an evangelical clergyman, Dan Craig from Hamilton. Moreover, Mary encouraged him to attend an evening class at which he mastered shorthand. Keir's daughter, Nan, later recorded that "he learnt to write shorthand, scratching the characters with the aid of his pit lamp on a slate blacked with smoke".[5]

CHRISTIAN AND TRADE UNIONIST

David Hardie could be a hard drinker and Mary was determined that her children would not adopt the same vice. Much of

Glasgow and beyond was gripped by a culture of heavy drinking. In response, the temperance movement came to the fore. Mary rejoiced when her eldest son joined the local branch, the Good Templars, and when he took the pledge at the age of seventeen. It was dominated by evangelical Christians and it was probably here that his spiritual interest was deepened, where he met Christians who became friends and lent him books.

Hardie entered into its activities, persuading individuals to take the pledge and lobbying government to control drinking outlets. An act of 1853 in Scotland had caused pubs to shut on Sundays and introduced a closing time of 11 p.m. on weekdays. But the movement wanted to go further, with some campaigners wanting local areas to decide whether they had pubs or not. Politically, temperance tended to receive the support of some Liberals, which would have confirmed Keir Hardie's preference for them against the Tories.

The temperance movement was no insular and punitive group. It also provided hotels, services, social activities, choirs, and dances where young men and women could meet. Later as a politician Hardie always favoured its hotels and eating places wherever he could. In his late teens and early twenties he was an attractive young man with a strong figure, red beard, and thick curly hair, who had several girlfriends. Then he met Lillias (known as Lillie) Wilson. Although the daughter of a publican she was a strong supporter of temperance. She had more education than most working-class girls, had trained as a dressmaker, and could read and write.

The young Hardie for all his seriousness did not confine himself to the Templars. His friend David Lowe recalls, "The radiance of youth itself made him sing the songs of his country, play the melodeon and banjo, follow football, and take part in concerts and dances like the collier lads around him."[6] So much for those biographers, who never knew him, who cast him as continually gloomy and moody.

By this time, Hardie was a fully fledged hewer and coal-cutter. He must have been aware of both physical and financial insecurity. At nearby Blantyre, over a hundred died following a pit explosion.

The Reform Act (1868) further extended the franchise. Some 60 per cent of males now had the vote. Thomas Burt and Alexander MacDonald, both former miners, became two of the first working-class MPs. If associated with the Liberals, they were called Lib–Labs. MacDonald, president of the new Miners' National Association and a Liberal MP in 1874, was much admired by Hardie. But, in the 1870s, a depression meant that wages were cut to 2s. a day. MacDonald found himself in the Liberal trap. He spoke in militant tones to the miners but dare not be too militant in the face of the Liberal pit-owners who paid his salary. He wanted to negotiate a sliding scale of wages and to limit coal output so that the price of coal and wages stayed high. The mine-owners were not impressed and wages were further reduced. Disappointment with MacDonald's failure was linked to accusations that he was in the pocket of the proprietors. He was also criticized for failing to bring in effective safety measures in the mines. The outcome was the formation of a Hamilton District Branch of the Lanarkshire Miners' Union and in 1878 Hardie agreed to be its secretary. The following year he was made corresponding secretary, which gave him contacts with other branches. Ayrshire and Lanarkshire were difficult places for trade unions because strikes or restriction of output could be broken by employers bringing in Irishmen as "blackleg" labour. Hardie's Templar friends tried to persuade him not to be involved in trade union work, saying that the odds were too great. But Hardie was committed to trade unions and took the posts.

In this period, Hardie became a Christian. In a scrap in his diary he penned: "Brought up an atheist – converted to Christianity in 1878." Carswell comments: "When he was seventeen the Moody and Sankey Mission arrived evoking an outburst of religious enthusiasm in the West of Scotland, especially among young men, that endured at fever heat for several years. In due course, Hardie succumbed to the general influence and became converted."[7] The Moody and Sankey missions were in 1874 and 1882 so Hardie, like others, may have been converted at a meeting inspired by, but not taken by, them. A number of his early biographers indicate that he went to an Evangelical Union church in Hamilton.

By his early twenties, Hardie had educated himself more than most miners, was a part of the temperance movement, had an interest in politics, and was a trade union official. Thousands of other miners had a similar background. What were the factors that particularly shaped Hardie's development?

THE SHAPING OF HIS DEVELOPMENT

First, his illegitimacy. Some biographers assert that Hardie felt a strong stigma about being born out of wedlock which drove him to achieve in order to prove his worth. His stepfather (usually referred to as his father) did call him "a bastard" when drunk but generally accepted and loved him. Hardie displayed no tension towards him and remained close until David Hardie's death. As an adult, Keir Hardie never denied nor publicized his illegitimacy. Those troubled by their illegitimacy often seek out their natural fathers in adulthood but Hardie showed no desire to do so. After all, in Lanarkshire 8.4 per cent of all births were outside marriage – it was not that unusual. Certainly, within the eventual Labour Party it was never regarded as a handicap. Ramsay MacDonald and other Labour politicians were also illegitimate. Being born out of wedlock was not a crucial factor in shaping the psychology of Keir Hardie.

Second, and much more important, was the influence of his mother Mary. Without her resourcefulness, the family would probably have finished up in the workhouse. She was an intelligent, hard-working, and principled woman, whose virtues could hardly have failed to influence her children. She wanted the best for her first-born son and also for her eight other children. She identified Keir's intelligence and serious mind and, as he grew older, she instilled into him the value of reading, taught him herself, found books, and encouraged him to attend evening courses. Fred Reid concluded, "Her patient, steady influence drew him away from the atheistical rebelliousness of his father towards the virtues of sobriety and self-help. She became a symbol to Hardie of everything that was best in working-class family life and motherhood generally."[8] Looking back, Hardie himself declared, "The face of the eident [busy], thrifty, hard-working mother and housewife who toils early and late for those she loves, acquires a sweet dignity which betimes I could almost worship."

Third, Hardie was profoundly moved by the suffering, the terrible housing, the illnesses, the poverty, and the unemployment that he witnessed every day of his life. It was not just poverty; it was also inequality. It enraged him that in a society where some enjoyed extremely high incomes and lived in luxury waited upon by servants, others were deprived of the basic necessities of life. He referred to "the idle rich", for often they or their offspring had not worked for their wealth but obtained it through inheritance or through investments and playing the stock market. Yet the idle rich often ignored the sufferings of those who laboured hard. From his sixteen years in the pits, Hardie saw hard-working people killed or maimed because rich mine-owners refused to keep safety rules. He knew men worn out by their forties and dismissed by employers who opposed attempts to bring in an eight-hour day. Such inequality divided people economically, socially, and spiritually.

Fourth, Hardie's early participation in the temperance movement was crucial. It provided an alternative social life to the drinking dens. In the Good Templars, he had his first contacts with educated and often radical members. One was Dr G. B. Clark, a Paisley industrialist who edited *The Good Templar Journal* and who was one of the first to call himself a socialist. Clarke clearly identified the potential of Hardie and encouraged him for many years.

As Graham Dale explains, "three social forces... were to have an impact on the development of the Labour Party" and he links the temperance movement with trade unions and co-operative societies.[9] The temperance movement was not just about getting individuals to sign the pledge. It also had a political edge, which campaigned through the press and public meetings to persuade MPs and councillors to take steps to close some outlets. Working-class people were given the opportunities to develop the skills of debating, campaigning, organizing, and speaking. Hardie's brothers used to hear him pacing on the floorboards as he practised his next talk. Many, such as George Lansbury, Willie Gallagher, Arthur Henderson, Philip Snowden, and Tom Johnston moved on to the political arena. Not least, most temperance groups gave equal status to women, which may well have determined Hardie's early commitment to female suffrage.

The temperance movement did attract many evangelical, often radical, Christians. Yet it was one of the few areas where Roman Catholics and Protestants could make common cause. This suited Hardie who, at a time of strong sectarianism, never attacked Catholics – although he could be critical of Irish immigrants whose arrival broke strikes.

Fifth, his reading was important. For one who rarely if ever went to school and who would have had little money to spare for books, Hardie's range of reading was astonishing. He consumed books in order to find answers to social questions, yet also obtained tremendous personal joy from them.

According to Hardie, two contrasting Scottish authors made

a profound impact on him. One was Robbie Burns, also from the Ayrshire countryside which Hardie grew to love, whose words Hardie sang and cited all his life. As Iain McLean puts it, "Hardie reacted instinctively to both the nationalistic and democratic strains in Burns' poetry."[10] In later life, Hardie represented English and Welsh constituencies in the Commons but he remained a devoted Scot and favoured Scottish home rule. In 1898, while at a conference in Birmingham, he went with Ramsay MacDonald to watch a football international at Aston Villa between England and Scotland. They found themselves in the midst of the English supporters but made their voices heard and cheered Scotland to a 2–0 win.

Even more, Hardie absorbed Burns' example of the low-born making good and his insistence on the basic equality of mankind. He rejoiced in "A Man's a Man for a' That" and would often repeat,

It's comin yet for a' that,
That Man to Man the world o'er,
Shall brothers be for a' that.

In addition, Hardie loved Burns' poetic pictures of Scottish countryside and life, along with his detailed observations of animals. After reading "On seeing a wounded hare limp by," Hardie said that he never threw a stone or showed cruelty to any animal. Certainly, several who knew him commented how he always had a friendly word for a mangy cat, while dogs straight away saw him as a friend.

The successful and wealthy Thomas Carlyle, who died in 1881, was very different from Burns. Anyone who has studied his works knows how difficult it is to understand his unique style of writing and of punctuation. Moreover, Hardie started with one of his most complex books, *Sartor Resartus*, which he read three times before he grasped the author's meaning.

Carlyle, although a reactionary in later life, had been an early critic of the commercialism and materialism beginning to dominate Britain in the nineteenth century. He attacked the wickedness of poverty in a land of plenty. Carlyle was not as strong on solutions and certainly socialism was not one of them. But Hardie seemed taken by Carlyle's insistence that hero figures would emerge to transform society. Perhaps he dreamed of being one. Not least, Hardie was taken by Carlyle's stories and arguments which showed the futility of war. As the sage showed, whatever the causes of wars, those who got killed were working-class young men who hardly knew what they were fighting about.

According to friends who wrote about him, Hardie also read John Ruskin, Henry George, John Bunyan, and John Stuart Mill; but noticeably no Marx. In terms of what he read, it was not economic analysis that turned Hardie into a trade unionist, political agitator and socialist. Rather it was books which revealed the huge social injustices in Britain and which suggested that change was possible.

What of the Bible? Caroline Benn reckons that Hardie did not possess one and was not "well grounded in the Scriptures".[11] Yet his friend and admirer William Stewart says that David and Mary Hardie, despite their atheistic views, had the Bible and *Pilgrim's Progress* on the same shelf as books opposed to religion. Even if not, Keir Hardie would surely have had access to Bibles in the Templars and in local churches. Hardie may not have been a theologian but his many uses of Scripture suggest he was well read in Christianity.

Sixth, several writers refer to the influence of the Covenanters on Hardie. The Covenanters were the strong Protestant Christians who resisted the imposition of bishops by the restored Stuart kings to supervise the Scottish church. After 1663, numbers of Covenanting ministers were ejected from their churches and held their services in the open air, where they were hunted and persecuted. Once in power, they were not exactly tolerant themselves.

Hardie rarely took much interest in issues of church governance. But, as a youngster, he was thrilled by reading about the adventures of Covenanters as they avoided capture and endured hardship for the sake of their beliefs. Moreover, he lived in the counties of Ayrshire and Lanarkshire where Covenanters had lived and he would have known the spots where they died.

One such spot was the battlefield of Aird's Moss. As a young union activist, Hardie spoke to miners on this slope. Later he recalled the miners marching there with their banners and wrote, "I thought that they were like the Covenanting armies of yore, gathering their strength to fight for freedom and justice and a new Covenant among working men."

A combination of personal experiences, the influence of his mother, the poverty and sufferings he witnessed, the discipline of the temperance movement, a range of reading, and the history of the Covenanters contributed to the man Hardie became. Some saw him as talented and motivated to bring about change. They were right.

CHAPTER 2

Journalist and Trade Unionist, 1879–86

During the 1880s, Keir Hardie worked as both a journalist and trade unionist. Both roles were to provide him with skills and experiences that shaped his future political activities.

The colliery manager at Pit no. 4 in Quarter, where Hardie was working, took action against the increasingly prominent young man. He told him, "We'll ha' no more damned Hardies in this pit." For good measure, he also sacked his two brothers who worked there, Alexander and Willie. No other pit would have him. Aged twenty-three, Keir Hardie's career as a miner was over. His later right-wing critic Donald Carswell commented that pit-owners weeded out "any man who showed speech-proclivities. Young Hardie soon made himself obnoxious in this respect" – and was dismissed.[1]

The Hardies moved to Cadzow on the outskirts of Hamilton, where Mary opened a small shop, while David Hardie found employment as a joiner. It seems that Hardie made some money as the local correspondent of the *Glasgow Weekly Mail*, one of the few papers to express support for miners.

Trade union leader

On 3 August 1879, Keir Hardie, aged twenty-three, and Lillie Wilson, aged seventeen, were married and moved into cramped accommodation. They had no honeymoon and the very next day Hardie spoke at a miners' meeting. It was the shape of their life to come. Pit-owners disliked him but many miners admired him and soon he was appointed miners' agent for the Lanarkshire miners.

As a young trade union leader at Hamilton District Branch, Hardie had a baptism of fire. The miners, tired of Alexander MacDonald's lack of success, wanted militant action, yet Hardie doubted if the union had sufficient funds for anything but a very short strike. The men insisted and a strike started in the autumn of 1879 and spread to other pits.

One of those who joined in was Robert (Bob) Smillie. Born in Belfast, he had moved to Larkhall and the pits as a boy and was soon a union official. Smillie says that he and Hardie had earlier played cricket against each other when he represented Larkhall while Hardie played for Quarter. But this was their first real meeting and they became friends for the rest of their lives. In his autobiography, Smillie shows that he was drawn by Hardie's devotion to the miners' cause, saying, "No man I ever knew worked so hard as Keir Hardie."[2] These strikes became known as "the tattie strike", as Hardie arranged credit to obtain potatoes for the men and their families. When the mine-owners and ironmasters brought in strike breakers, it collapsed.

Alexander MacDonald had disagreed with the strike and was angry that he – a veteran trade union leader and now an MP – had had to argue with Hardie in public. He promised the miners he would see to paying off their tattie debts on condition that Hardie was sent packing. Hardie did not make the men decide; he thought it in their best interests that he left. The breach between the two was never healed and it was Hardie's first public break with a Lib–Lab leader.

Hardie and Lillie moved to Cumnock to a two-room house in Waterside Place, where their miner friends had left food and furniture as a welcoming gift. The Ayrshire miners wanted him as their paid organizer. But the employers were fiercely against him and several miners were told they would be sacked if they invited Hardie into their cottages.

The Hardies were to live in Cumnock for the rest of their lives. By the end of the year, the Hardies had no income. But they did now have a son, Jamie. Keir worked for a while as an insurance agent for a London firm but his earnings were meagre.

JOURNALIST

Then came a turning point. The minister of the Cumnock Congregational Church, which the Hardies had started to attend, was a part-time reporter for the *Cumnock News*, a part of the *Ardrossan and Saltcoats Herald*. Ill health made him give up the post and he recommended Hardie, whose abilities were soon recognized by the editor. Arthur Guthrie was both editor and owner of the paper, a staunch Liberal who liked to stand up to the Tory aristocrats and landowners who held so much power in the area. The minister never returned, so Hardie had a secure job at £1 a week.

From April 1882 to 1887 Hardie wrote news and a regular column mainly about miners and mines, which he signed "Trapper". He was writing for a Liberal readership and a Liberal editor and, not surprisingly, identified with the Liberal Party himself. Initially he stressed the virtues of co-operation rather than conflict between bosses and workers. Then he praised the importance of co-operative and temperance movements made up of working-class people which would "elevate the working classes of this country into a position of high social comfort and independence". On the other hand, he regularly attacked pit-owners who ignored the sufferings of miners and their families.

And not only industry. His interest in education featured in the paper when he questioned whether the Education Act (1872) was being fully implemented. At an early stage in his journalism, he became a supporter of women's suffrage. In 1884 one of his articles called upon the Liberals to debate the abolition of the House of Lords. He was a Liberal, but one wanting the party to be more radical.

Fred Reid accuses Keir Hardie of deserting working-class life to become a middle-class journalist writing for a middle-class readership. It was impossible for Hardie to be a miner – no company would employ him. Yet his loyalty to miners had endured. He retained his membership of the trade union. At times, he and his family were reduced to near poverty. Even Reid acknowledges that "he helped at least two working miners to bring legal actions against their employers and letters praising him for this appeared in the press".[3] He sometimes gave direct assistance to miners who could not cope with financial and other problems.

The journalistic years were significant for Hardie. His pseudonym did not hide his identity and he became well known in central and western Scotland. He obtained publishing and writing skills which were of enormous value later when he launched mining and Labour papers. Not least, his writings made him think and he began to question whether the Liberal Party, along with its handful of working-class MPs, would ever bring in radical social change.

The Hardies had settled in Cumnock, a small town which had grown to a population of over 3,000 following the coming of the railways. The main industries were coal-mines and an ironworks. In 1882, they rented a two-room tenement in Barrhill

Road, which had a small garden that the couple enjoyed. Their first son Jamie was followed by Sarah, Agnes (known as Nan), and Duncan. Their home was soon overcrowded.

Keir Hardie grew to love Cumnock. Almost immediately he entered into its civic activities. His enthusiastic involvement in the branch of the Good Templars resulted, according to the press, in a fourfold increase in membership. It appears that Hardie was prepared to tramp around local villages to recruit working-class people into the movement. He participated in a benefit evening for the poor and a free breakfast and supper for the aged. In 1883, he was promoted to Grand Worthy Chief of the Templars' Lodge.

Somehow he also found the time to run free evening classes in shorthand for workers. Notes at the Cumnock archives show that in 1885 he was elected a member of the Auchinleck School Board. Auchinleck was a few miles from Cumnock but Hardie was well known there for his temperance and previous trade union work. He was concerned that pupils were being charged money, which he considered to contradict the Education Act (1872). The handwritten minutes of a meeting on 7 September 1886 record that Hardie could not be present but had sent a letter proposing that where parents had three children at one school only the two youngest should pay fees. The minutes stated, "Mr Hardie not being present the motion was not moved and accordingly fell to the ground." In December he presented his motion in person but it was not carried. In 1886 he stood as a candidate for Cumnock Town Council but was defeated.

CHURCH ACTIVITY

He gave much time and energy to the church. Surprisingly, three of his main biographers – William Stewart, Iain McLean, and Kenneth Morgan – say little about his membership of and struggles within the Cumnock Congregational Church, while Margaret Cole says nothing at all about them, although she does mention that Hardie was "an undogmatic Christian".[4] The Hardies joined on 19 July 1882. It was the minister here who found Keir Hardie his job in journalism but then retired because of ill health.

He was replaced by the Reverend Andrew Scott, who soon found himself in dispute with some of the deacons. In the Cumnock archive is an article written in 1981 by James Drummond, whose grandfather Adam Drummond had been the secretary of the church and who retained the minute book from the time of this church feud.

Adam Drummond had a large family house, a small foundry, and a blacksmith's shop, all of which prospered. Initially Adam Drummond and his wife, Jane, got on well with the Hardies. Drummond was president of the local Liberal Association, a contributor to the Liberal press, and a local agent for the great Liberal leader William Gladstone. Both Drummond and Hardie supported the Liberal Party but also believed that the church should take an active part in social matters. In a bitterly cold winter, they pioneered job creation schemes by organizing the jobless into such tasks as clearing snow off the streets and constructing a flushing pond on the River Glaisnock to give the town a clean water supply. They paid the workers from the street-lighting fund – James Drummond says this was probably illegal. Both Drummond and Hardie were ardent temperance men and persuaded the town council to have the back door of every public house bricked up to curb the illegal sale of drink outside licensing hours. Both were enthusiastic church participants, attending weekday as well as Sunday meetings, with Hardie often preaching in other churches.

But then the Drummond–Hardie friendship began to fall apart. In January 1884, Hardie presided at a Burns Supper. He proposed a long toast to the immortal poet, which was drunk in Turner's non-alcoholic cordial. This did not soften the criticisms of those who regarded the gathering as unspiritual and Burns as a drunkard. The leading critic was Jane Drummond. James Drummond recalled that his grandmother disapproved of many things: picture-houses, Sunday newspapers, dance bands, church raffles, and most of Burns' poetry. Hardie then made matters worse by giving a talk to a debating society on "Was Burns a Drunkard?" and concluding that he was not.

Matters came to a head when Drummond and some other deacons considered that the Reverend Andrew Scott had dealt too leniently with a member, Mr Elliot, who had been drunk. Despite his temperance views, Hardie sided with the minister. He considered that the attitude of Drummond and his supporters was too much about condemnation and too little about forgiveness. Keir and Lillie then went out of their way to show kindness to Mr and Mrs Elliot.

The following Sunday, Hardie uncharacteristically stayed at home. He wrote in his diary on Monday 18 February, "Did not go to church on Sunday as I had heard that it was proposed to put me on a deputation to visit Mr Elliot." There was no way out. In his absence, the congregation voted that Hardie should visit Mr Elliot. Hardie made up his mind. The Reverend Andrew Scott fell ill under the attacks on him and Hardie was asked to lead the Wednesday prayer meeting. He wrote, "I read 2nd chapter of James." This chapter condemns the rich who have little sympathy for the poor. The deacons glared at him. A few days later they decided to dismiss the minister and gave him notice. Hardie accompanied the Reverend Andrew Scott when he appealed unsuccessfully to senior deacons in Glasgow. They seemed to acknowledge that the minister was in the right but said he would still have to go. As Hardie put it, their attitude was that "those who were opposed to him [Scott] were the pillars of the church [financially] and should be given in to". He added, "Principle is overthrown to please Mammon. This may be Christianity but I will have none of it." A few days later, the Hardies' second child, Sarah, was baptized at the church. Apart from the Hardies, the Scotts and the Elliots were the only ones present.

The unsympathetic deacons evicted the Reverend Andrew Scott and his wife from the manse three months before the date Hardie had negotiated with them. He promptly resigned from the church. The affair, to Hardie, was about the way Christianity should be interpreted and lived. Further, by breaking with church leaders, who were also prominent, middle-class Liberals, Hardie demonstrated that he was not prepared to curry their favour in order to secure his political future as a Liberal.

The minutes kept by Adam Drummond record that over forty members resigned, their stated reason being: "We object to the high-handed arbitrary manner in which the Reverend Andrew Scott has been forced to resign as pastor of the church without any reason whatsoever."

With the dissenting members of the Congregational church, Hardie formed an Evangelical church which met in a rented hall. The Evangelical Union was established in 1842 when the Reverend James Morrison was accused of heresy by the older Presbyterian churches on four grounds. These were that he proclaimed that God loved all men, that Christ died for all, that the Holy Spirit strives with all men, and that all may be saved if they turn to Christ. The accusers were in the Calvinist tradition and held that God predestined some to eternal life and some to eternal death. Morrison rejoiced in being guilty of these charges. His Evangelical Union preached that Christ welcomed all repentant sinners. It grew to be a small but significant denomination which, as Professor Smout says, attracted "artisans and miners".[5] Hardie declared in his diary when the Cumnock Evangelical Church was starting, "My heart rejoices at the prospect as I do love the Evangelical Union."

Hardie became one of the leaders in the church and sometimes preached there, sometimes in other churches and in the open air. He also ministered to the sick and dying. Soon the church had a choir of fifty. He records that one social in the hall went on until 11 p.m., after which he and Mrs Elliot swept up and then consecrated the church in prayer.

The numbers and collections at the Congregational church decreased. But it was too rich to be in danger of closing – and still stands today. In fact, the Evangelical church was in much more financial danger, as it had few rich supporters. Nonetheless, some Congregational deacons abused Hardie in the local press. Hardie's wish to be in a working-class church, and his readiness to oppose the deacons, counters those who say that he deserted his working-class roots and that he befriended Liberals for the sake of his career.

The Cumnock Evangelical Union church apparently flourished for some years. In 1890 the Evangelical Union movement united with other denominations. It is not known for how long Hardie continued as a regular church-goer. Once he became a travelling politician, he was often away from home at weekends. But this did not mean he ceased to be a Christian. Far from it. His friend David Lowe wrote, "Throughout his life, Hardie never lost his faith he preached in those days."[6]

Morgan does not go into detail about Hardie's religious beliefs and activities yet concedes that they shaped his politics: "His Christianity was highly flexible, a religion of humanity with little doctrinal content, utopian, romantic, outward-looking, democratic and egalitarian. Its ultimate justification lay in the vision of the true believer and in the priesthood of all mankind, pledged to the coming of 'the Christ that is to be'. On such a basis, rather than on hard-headed economic analysis, was Hardie's socialism to be founded."[7]

HOME LIFE

What about Hardie's home life? The diary that has already been cited was one he decided to keep for 1884. Before starting it, he wrote, "I must confess that I waste a good deal of time in desultory reading." He resolved to put aside "2 hours every morning to study before I breakfast". He opted for French and arithmetic, of which he admitted, "I know absolutely nothing."

The completed pages, few as they are, reveal the pattern of Keir and Lillie's lives. His entry for Tuesday 1 January 1884 was: "Brought in New Year with silent prayer at watch meeting in church vestry. Very pleasant meeting." On Wednesday 6 January he recorded: "Our second child born this morning between 6 and 7. Lillie was ill all night but after birth got wonderfully well and continued so all day." The baby girl was their second child, Sarah. On Thursday 7 January, he told how, after being elected to the chair at a Good Templar meeting, he lost his temper over a trifling matter within five minutes.

The diaries then have fairly full accounts of the dismissal of the Reverend Andrew Scott and Hardie's siding with him. On Saturday 15 March, he made an entry about a child of five apparently drowned in the River Lugar. He penned, "Dr says he had been strangled not drowned... My heart bleeds for poor parents but trust they can look with the eye of faith and see their little one Safe in the Arms of Jesus."

The diary, which unfortunately did not last long, reflects a home- and community-loving man. He always recorded what time they went to bed, what the weather was like, and often how the garden was doing. Apart from his job as a journalist, which involved a good deal of travel, he was fully taken up with local activities.

Critics have argued that Keir and Lillie were not a satisfactory partnership and that Hardie frequently left her at home alone with the children. Emrys Hughes, Hardie's son-in-law, who drew heavily on the memories of Nan Hardie, gives another perspective. Writing of the period when Hardie had been sacked from the pits, Lillie was pregnant, and money was in short supply, he commented: "They were right up against it. Lillie Hardie did not grumble or complain. They had decided to face life together and she would stand by and give encouragement to her man. She did not grumble or reproach him. The bonds of sympathy and understanding between them grew."[8] Certainly they went to church together and Garth Lean writes about their early days when together: "The young couple gave counsel on the problems of the pit, comfort to hearts bitter in bereavement, material help to those fallen on hard days."[9] It is worth mentioning that, although Lillie's father is always spoken of as a publican, his occupation on the marriage certificate is given as miner. His time as a miner may well explain his daughter's sympathies for them. Caroline Benn adds that Hardie was "helpful and sometimes took over the children for an afternoon".[10] But a heavy load was placed on Lillie's shoulders.

Hardie in 1886 seemed settled as a journalist, church leader, and family man. Then, at the end of 1886, the Ayrshire miners invited him to be their union secretary. He accepted at £75 a year, supplemented by another £5 for working part time for the newly formed Scottish Miners' Federation. He was soon working hard for a moderate income in a job less secure than that of a journalist: hardly the actions of a man who deserted the working class for a career with the middle class.

EMERGENCE OF SOCIALISM

Lastly, these were the years of the emergence of socialism – whatever its definition – by movements, groups and individuals. Geoffrey Foote in his history of the Labour Party states that "it was in the turmoil of the 1880s that the different and conflicting views which were to make up the ideas of British socialism were formed and fought over".[11] Certainly, there are indications that Hardie was drawn to socialism, but this is not to say that he subscribed to it at this stage.

Karl Marx was well known in Britain, although his works were not widely read. Probably, Hardie had not read them. But Marx's attacks on capitalism and his belief in the inevitability of its demise did attract many followers and, on the first anniversary of his death in 1884, a huge crowd assembled at his grave at Highgate cemetery.

Henry Hyndman had read Marx. He was a wealthy Old Etonian and Oxford graduate who always dressed as a gentleman. In 1881 he formed a group called the Democratic Foundation, which distributed a booklet, *England for All*, which used Marx's writings without using his name. Not surprisingly, Marx was miffed. Hyndman thought there would be a revolution but that it should be led by himself. For all his faults, he was an outstanding speaker and debater, who drew many to the party he formed in 1884, the Social Democratic Federation (the SDF). He advocated the abolition of capitalism along with the nationalization of the means of production to end the exploitation of the working class. As Reid explains, the SDF "produced the first socialist critique seen in England of the trade unions as bastions of privileged workers whose organized interests could and often did diverge from the interests of the working class in emancipation from insecurity and poverty".[12] As mentioned, Hyndman attracted many to the party, including William Morris and Marx's daughter, Eleanor. Most left, put off by the egotism and dictatorial style of Henry Hyndman.

Very different from the SDF was the Fabian Society which was led by middle-class intellectuals, in particular Sidney and Beatrice Webb and George Bernard Shaw. The Fabians were opposed to any form of violent revolution to bring about political change and advocated making reasoned arguments for socialism. These arguments usually concluded that the state should promote services and greater public ownership. They did not set up a party but wanted to permeate existing parties. They were not enthusiastic about drawing working-class people into their society. Keir Hardie was never a Fabian enthusiast although he later co-operated with George Bernard Shaw, who admired him.

Hardie went to hear, and later met, the American Henry George, author of a popular book, *Progress and Poverty*. He proposed a tax on all land, with the proceeds going to the poor. He won a following in Scotland, especially among the rural poor, who worked the land for little gain.

Cumnock certainly was not the centre of socialism. Nonetheless, Keir Hardie did meet individuals with socialist leanings. In 1886, he made contact with William Small, the general secretary of the Lanarkshire miners for a while, who had socialist leanings. Within Cumnock itself lived Alexander Barrowman and James Neil, who were Liberals but moving toward socialism. Barrowman was a mining engineer who participated in the Cumnock Literary and Debating Society. Neil, a miner, joined the SDF in 1885 during a visit to London. He purchased its journal *Justice*, which he may well have lent to Hardie.

At this time in London, George Lansbury was walking the same path as Keir Hardie. Born in 1859, he was reared in conditions of social hardship and with little education. Like Hardie, he was a Christian who was active in the temperance movement. Like Hardie, his early political leanings favoured the Liberals and, indeed, he showed his skills as one of their election agents. He soon perceived that the Liberal Party exploited people like him and he was persuaded by the SDF that socialism was the means to alter society for the best.

The influential Liberal MP Sir Samuel Montagu regarded Lansbury as one of the working-class men who could be a Liberal MP and so win working-class votes. He promised Lansbury a salary and a seat in the Commons if he stayed with the Liberals. He added that he was a better socialist than Lansbury, as he gave away a tenth of his income. Lansbury's famous reply was: "We socialists want to prevent you getting the nine-tenths. We do not believe in rich and poor and charity."[13]

The date when Hardie and Lansbury first met is not known. Lansbury became an evangelist for socialism and often spoke in Glasgow and Paisley. In later years, Paisley socialists wanted him as their parliamentary candidate but he wanted to stay in east London. They probably met in the late 1880s and found they had similar experiences and ideas which culminated in a belief in socialism.

It cannot be said that trade unions were advocates of socialism at this time. Of course, there was no Labour Party, and trade unions (if they supported any party) mainly identified with the Liberals, although a number sided with the Tories. Their strategy was to find favour with these parties in order to gain legislative support – as over safety and work conditions. Finding favour could mean restricting strikes and militant action against employers.

However, in the 1880s some individual members of trade unions looked seriously at socialism. Keir Hardie was always a trade unionist. George Lansbury in 1889 joined the National Union of Municipal and General Workers and remained a member for the rest of his life. Tom Mann was originally a miner and then a tool maker. Once he became an engineer, he perceived that unemployment was not the result of workers' fecklessness and that the Liberals had no answers. For a while, Mann was in the SDF until he could stand Hyndman no longer. In 1887 Hardie and Mann met in London and must have discussed the relevance of socialism to trade unions. Two years later, along with Ben Tillett and Will Thorne, Mann famously supported a dock strike in London.

Caroline Benn comments that the nonconformist churches, frequently assumed to be the bedrock of support for socialism and later the Labour Party, were often a reactionary force. She is right that some chapels became dominated by wealthy industrialists who were opposed to state intervention which might alter the so-called free market. But she is not wholly correct. F. B. Meyer was a Baptist famous for his preaching, books on holiness, and participation in the evangelical Keswick Convention. Less known is that from 1878 to 1887 he built up a working-class church in Leicester and undertook an extensive and successful work among discharged prisoners. In 1892, he took on the declining Christ Church in Lambeth, even though it meant a much reduced salary. Again, he established many welfare projects but soon concluded that charity was not sufficient and that government intervention was required to tackle unemployment, poor housing, and pensions. As president of the Baptist Union, he toured the country complaining about the low wages of women and criticized Christians who made handsome profits by investing in firms which treated women badly. He declared that Britain should be a less competitive and a more co-operative society. Meyer was always a Liberal but, in the days before there was a Labour Party, his secretary said, he was "practically a Christian socialist".[14]

Meyer's colleague John Clifford, another Baptist, was an out-and-out socialist. The claim is not that most churches were socialist or even overtly political. Rather there were numbers of Christians who drew their socialism from their Christianity. Keir Hardie was one.

In 1886, Hardie was still a Liberal. But his interest in socialism was increasing and the question was whether he could reconcile it with being a Liberal.

CHAPTER 3

From Scottish Liberals to Scottish Labour, 1887–88

In his book *The Origins of the Labour Party*, the historian Henry Pelling explains that, despite the widening of the franchise which meant that in many constituencies working-class voters were in a majority, "the working class still had no direct part in the government of the country" in the 1880s.[1] Standing for the Commons cost a considerable amount of money and MPs received no salaries. Trade unions were not united enough or organized enough to sponsor their own MPs, even if they had the desire and money. The Fabian Society did not regard itself as a political party. The most prominent socialist group, the Social Democratic Federation (SDF), probably never had more than a thousand members at any one time and lacked financial resources.

The only way working-class men could become MPs was if one of the two major parties, Tories and Liberals, undertook their expenses. The Liberals, in particular, were prepared to do so in a few cases in order to attract working-class votes. Many working-class voters, especially in Scotland, did favour the Liberals, whose leader William Gladstone had championed the extension of those who could vote.

In the 1874 election two ex-miners, Thomas Burt and Alexander MacDonald, became Liberal MPs. In the 1880 election, won by the Liberals, a third was added in the person of Henry Broadhurst of the Trade Union Congress (TUC). The difficulty for these MPs was that they had to side with a party which had many objections to any state interference with the free market. Thus their party loyalty could make them oppose, for instance, legislation to enforce an eight-hour day in all mines. There were other MPs with sympathies for the working class but Pelling concluded that "the acceptance of Liberal political guidance of the Labour leadership was never more complete than in 1880" and added that "there were few Labour leaders who regarded the establishment of an entirely independent workers' party as a practical possibility".[2] But then came Keir Hardie. At this time he was a Scot who had never been outside Scotland and a supporter of the Liberal Party. A Scottish Liberal. But all this was to change in the mid- and late 1880s.

POLITICS AND TRADE UNIONS

From 1886 Hardie worked energetically as a trade union official for the Ayrshire miners and the Scottish Miners' Federation. In one year he spoke at seventy-seven meetings and travelled 6,000 rail miles in his part-time job with the latter. Significantly, he did not just concentrate on recruiting more members. He campaigned about the lack of safety in the mines and wage issues. He also advocated an eight-hour day and called for a national superannuation scheme to protect miners in times of trouble. His political horizons were widening. So were his geographical ones, as he made his first trips to England to a miners' conference in Manchester and the following year to one in Birmingham. He realized how divided the various miners' unions were and how difficult it would be to organize a national strike. He was glad to be back every day with working-class people, which did not happen when he was a journalist. His commitment to the working class was one of his strongest features.

At the end of 1886, his friend Robert Smillie led the Lanarkshire miners into a strike. Hardie had his doubts about the wisdom of the strike but loyally supported it. The pit-owners – perhaps because of the creation of the Scottish Miners' Federation – acted in unison. In February 1887, they refused to speak to the union and brought in blacklegs from Glasgow, protected by large numbers of policemen, to work in the mines. Some miners reacted with rioting. At Blantyre a few looted a food van for their starving families and the Hussars from Glasgow rode in and arrested men indiscriminately. In Ayrshire, police were sent to stop Hardie going to miners' cottages to encourage them to stop work in support of the Lanarkshire men. The strike failed. As never before, Hardie saw that the state was on the side of the mine-owners, even to the extent of inflicting violence. As he pointed out, sixteen pit-owners were MPs.

What was the reaction of the Lib–Lab MPs, the former miners? Not much. Hardie's patience with the MPs who were supposed to speak for the miners was wearing thin. Later in 1887, he attended his first TUC conference at Swansea as a delegate for the Ayrshire miners. He was not well known outside Scotland, but the audience soon heard his voice when he publicly criticized Henry Broadhurst MP, secretary of the Parliamentary Committee of the TUC. Broadhurst had not voted in the Commons for the eight-hour day and had also given his support in a by-election to a Liberal, Sir John Brunner, who had a bad reputation as an employer and in whose company Broadhurst had shares. Few delegates supported Hardie and, at the close of the conference, Charles Fenwick, a miners' leader in the chair, insinuated that Hardie was a revolutionary who would soon fade away.

But Hardie was not the type to fade away. Bruce Glasier was a Scot who, although trained as an architect, was often unemployed. He met Hardie at political meetings and they became firm friends and Glasier subsequently often wrote about him. He later wrote that Hardie's challenge to the working-class MPs at the conference was "the first authentic note for Independent Labour Representation in that assembly".[3]

Hardie did not cease his attacks. At other meetings and the next TUC conference, he stated that Liberal mine-owners and factory-owners were not interested in improving the wages and work conditions of workers and that the Lib–Lab MPs sided with the Liberal Party.

Also in the eventful year of 1887, with funds from the Scottish Miners' Federation and some from his own pocket, he started a monthly journal of sixteen pages called *The Miner, A Journal for Underground Workers*. The timing was good in that universal primary education meant that more miners could read. The Scottish Miners' Federation distributed it, although Hardie carefully retained the ownership.

Hardie wrote much of the content himself. It gave him the space verbally to attack the Lib–Lab MPs. By this time, eleven working-class men were MPs, all of whom accepted the Liberal whip. He stated, "But what difference will it make to me that I have a working man representing me in Parliament, if he is a dumb dog who dare not bark and will follow the leader under any circumstances? There is something even more desirable than the return of working men to Parliament and that is to give working men a definite programme to fight for when they get there and to warn them that if they haven't the courage to stand up in the House of Commons and say what they would say in a miners' meeting, they must make room for someone else who will." He then proceeded to outline a programme to include payment of MPs, adult suffrage, free education, the nationalization of land, railways, mines, and mineral rights, a legal eight-hour day, and the compulsory building of houses for working people.

Kenneth Morgan argues that, at this time, Hardie was still thinking of "a Labour pressure-group, not an independent party".[4] James Maxton, who knew Hardie and who later became a prominent MP for the Independent Labour Party, would have disagreed. He wrote that, in *The Miner*, Hardie "taught the people that their poverty was a man-made thing, and that they themselves had it within them to remove that poverty". He added that by this time "the idea of creating a Labour Party had already taken hold of Hardie's mind".[5] It is worth noting that the general election of 1885 brought eighty-six Irish Nationalists to the Commons. Skilfully wielded together by Charles Parnell, they became a significant force. Probably Hardie foresaw the day when a Labour Party would do the same. Indeed, from the contents of *The Miner*, Emrys Hughes concluded that "Hardie had become an avowed socialist, declared war on the old leaders and was advocating an independent Labour Party."[6] Nonetheless, it seems that this was a transitional stage, with Hardie both within the Liberal fold yet making the case to leave.

Hardie did not limit his travels to conferences. In 1887 he also visited London with the intention of joining the SDF. He attended its meetings and was upset by the heavy drinking that went on. He discovered that Hyndman was opposed to trade unions in which members joined together to improve their work conditions. Not least, he disliked the calls that were made for violent action. To digress, Hardie's opposition to violence had a strong influence on his contemporaries and drew a number of Christians to his side.

Hardie decided not to join the SDF. But his socialism was boosted by an introduction to Marx's collaborator, Friedrich Engels, and Marx's daughter, Eleanor. They approved of Hardie's rejection of Hyndman, and Eleanor later wrote to a friend praising Hardie and wondering how he, Lillie, and four children survived on £80 a year.

Back in Scotland, Hardie had prepared his yearly report as secretary of the Scottish Miners' Federation for November 1887. It showed that the federation had grown to 13,000 members, although, it must be added, the various unions were still not united in action. He did not deliver the report in person, as his two-year-old daughter, Sarah, had fallen seriously ill, apparently with scarlet fever. As Caroline Benn points out, "Whenever there was a serious illness in the family, Hardie dropped everything and took a full hand in the nursing and bedside sitting."[7] Sadly Sarah died, leaving Keir and Lillie devastated.

THE MID LANARK BY-ELECTION

Earlier in 1887, Hardie had hurried to a colliery disaster in Udston, Lanarkshire, in which eighty-five men died. Some of the men had been his personal friends. He felt bitter anger toward the mine-owners, who had neglected safety procedures. He also bore an enormous work-load, and had little money: then came his daughter's death. No wonder there was often sadness in his eyes, no wonder that in his early thirties Hardie looked much older than his age. Nonetheless, as Pelling commented, he was still a "stocky, heavily bearded young Scot with the deep piercing eyes which won attention".[8] Certainly, many miners were drawn to him and the Ayrshire ones adopted him as their candidate for the next general election. Hardie appears to have concluded that he needed a wider political scene to bring about change. Then in March 1888 a by-election became necessary at Mid Lanark, the very area in which Hardie had spent many of his early years.

Apparently he had not shed all his Liberal garments, as he sought nomination from the Liberal Party. Instead, local Liberals chose a London barrister, J. W. Philipps. The Liberal hierarchy sensed that Hardie would still stand and capture some voters. A top official from London offered him a seat elsewhere at the next election and a substantial salary. "It was characteristic of Hardie", Pelling states, "that he at once refused this offer, which, though likely to have secured his future, would have involved the abandonment of the miners' cause in Lanarkshire."[9]

So Hardie, with nomination papers signed by miners – which horrified *The Times* – became the Labour and Home Rule candidate. The addition was to show the sizeable number of Irish residents in the constituency where he stood on the question of home rule for Ireland. A number of bodies indicated their support. The Scottish Home Rule Association showed its approval with a letter from its London-based secretary, Ramsay MacDonald. This is the first known contact between Hardie and MacDonald who, after Hardie's death, was to become Labour's first prime minister. But the Home Rule Association had little influence in Mid Lanark. Backing also came from the Labour Electoral Association, which had been formed by the TUC to coordinate local bodies promoting working-class candidates. Its secretary, T. R. Threlfall, initially spoke of a contribution of £400 to Hardie's election expenses but then urged him to accept the Liberal offer of a safe seat elsewhere – much safer than Mid Lanark. When Hardie refused, Threlfall left.

A more important recruit to Hardie's side was John Ferguson, a Glasgow councillor who was leader in the Irish National League, which worked to register the votes of Irish residents likely to vote for candidates who favoured home rule.

What was Hardie's programme? Benn says that it "erred on the side of conservatism".[10] True he said he would vote Liberal in the Commons but his programme contained radical, even socialist proposals, which would anger many Liberal MPs. He opened his election address: "You will see that the working men of Scotland have no representatives to urge their claims. It is in order to remedy this admitted grievance that I now claim your support." He went on to urge the nationalization of land and the abolition of the Lords. He described the national expenditure on royalty as "a disgrace". He concluded, "I ask you therefore to return to Parliament a man of yourselves who being poor can feel for the poor."

The *Glasgow Herald,* covering one of his speeches at Cambuslang, reported that he spoke on behalf of the Labour Party which would one day replace the Liberal Party. It went on: "He looked at the faces of the gathering before him and he saw the death-mark on nine out of every ten of them. They knew they were being poisoned in the pit with foul air; they knew that their fate at the end of their working days was the open door of the workhouse. The only solution was for them to form a party." This was hardly "erring on the side of conservatism".

Hardie and his supporters had a difficult task in a large constituency and had nothing like the human, financial, and transport resources of their opponents. The miners who backed him were limited by the long hours they worked and their lack of mobility. Yet socialists, trade unionists, and radicals from outside came to campaign with him.

Particular mention must be made of the presence of Robert Cunninghame Graham, who had spent his early years rearing cattle in South America before returning in 1884 to take over his father's estates in Dunbartonshire. An expert horseman and a flamboyant figure, he was elected MP for North West Lanark in 1886. In the Commons he expressed his sympathies for the working class. Indeed, the tone of his speeches caused Benn to call him "a socialist, the first ever to be elected to Parliament".[11] In December 2008, BBC2 showed a documentary about Cunninghame Graham's extraordinary life called *The Adventures of Don Roberto*. Hearing of Hardie, he turned up at his house on a superb black horse. Hardie invited him in and was convinced of his sincerity, and they became close friends.

Cunninghame Graham took Hardie to see Parliament and educated him on how government worked. Hardie educated him on what working-class life was really like and even took him down a coal-mine.

Critics of Hardie have said that he made few friendships. True, he was not gregarious and was not one who liked dinner parties and social events. But he did make a number of lasting friendships. Some of his friends have already been mentioned and others were to include George Barnes, the Benson family, Rose Davies, David Lowe, the Hughes family, the Pankhurst family, Frank Smith, and Philip Snowden.

The influx of his friends such as Robert Smillie, Cunninghame Graham, and others from further afield at the election was used by his opponents to sneer about outsiders taking over and insinuate that Hardie was controlled from London. This was hardly justified considering that the Liberal and Conservative candidates were from outside, while Hardie was the only local one.

Liberals spread the rumour that Hardie was being paid with Tory gold: hardly likely considering that he had turned down the offer of Liberal gold and a future seat. Nonetheless, Kenneth Morgan believes that Hardie probably was funded by H. H. Champion, an eccentric Tory socialist, who saw working-class candidates as a means of dividing the Liberal vote. Hardie did receive £100 from Margaret Harkness, who wrote socialist novels. Small amounts would have come from his local supporters.

Even with these donations, Hardie's campaign lacked money.

On polling day in April, the Liberals and Tories had gigs and carriages to get voters to the polls. Hardie had none. Ferguson did not win over the Irish vote. Not surprisingly Hardie finished bottom of the poll with just 617 votes (8 per cent of the total); the Liberals won easily with 3,847 votes.

The Mid Lanark by-election had focused national attention on Hardie. He now turned defeat into apparent victory. He toured the constituency to thank his supporters. He addressed a manifesto to the "Gallant Six Hundred", saying, "Your vote marks a turning point in history. You have raised the 'conditions of the people' question to a first place… Perfect your organisation; educate your fellows; look to the register; spread the light, and the future is yours."

James Maxton MP, looking back some fifty years later, wrote: "The significance of the contest, however, lay in the break which was made by the working class with their traditional association with the Liberal Party."[12] Morgan agrees: "His experience at Mid Lanark strengthened his view that the only sure route for the working-class, as well as for himself, was the path of independence."[13] It should not be thought that Hardie was the only one moving in this direction. The SDF, some miners in the west of Scotland, and political agitators such as Bruce Glasier thought the same and may well have influenced Hardie. But Hardie's access to a published journal, his many speeches, and his growing reputation made him the central figure.

THE SCOTTISH LABOUR PARTY

But Hardie at Mid Lanark was not a member of the Labour Party. No such party existed. His next step was to create one: the Scottish Labour Party (the SLP). In May 1888 Hardie called a preliminary meeting in Glasgow to elect a small committee to organize a conference which assembled in August with Cunninghame Graham in the chair. The audience was made up of representatives of various political and protest groups plus miners. A constitution was approved, while Cunninghame Graham was elected president, with Dr G. B. Clark MP, a long-time supporter of Hardie and a cotton manufacturer from Paisley, as vice-president. In the chair was Shaw Maxwell, a former parliamentary candidate for the Scottish Land Restoration League. The treasurer was John Ferguson and Hardie was the secretary.

A programme for the SLP was agreed, which included the prohibition of the liquor traffic (both Hardie and Clark were strong temperance men), the abolition of the House of Lords, the nationalization of land, minerals, railways, waterways, and tramways, free education, boards to provide food for children, and taxes on incomes over £300. The programme had socialist elements but did not call for the end of capitalism. Hardie did not want a narrow socialist party on the lines of the SDF. He wanted a broad church which would attract radicals, dissatisfied liberals, trade unionists, social reformers concerned about the plight of children, and socialists. He did want a party that was quite distinct from the Liberals and he went out of his way to welcome middle-class members who were committed to the cause of the working class. At this juncture, Hardie finally resigned from the Liberal Party.

The SLP endured for six years until it merged with the Independent Labour Party in 1894. Initially its membership did increase thanks to Hardie's efforts. It attempted to intervene in local elections and by-elections with no great success. There were disagreements with some members who still wanted to build bridges with the Liberals and John Ferguson was expelled for his public advocacy of the Liberal Party. Its greatest failure was to obtain any trade union backing except for the miners: the railway and dockers' unions declined to join. Nonetheless a new political party separate from the Tories and Liberals had been established.

Becoming a socialist

Given all this activity, it is easy to forget that Hardie was still a trade union worker. The Ayrshire miners did gain small wage increases for which he could take some credit. Unfortunately, there is little evidence of what else he did. However, some papers in the Cumnock archives reveal not only that he continued to work vigorously with miners but also that he encouraged lace-workers and carpet-workers in Ayrshire to form trade unions. When carpet-weavers went on strike, Hardie travelled to encourage them and participated in the negotiations which led to a settlement.

Hardie's activities in the 1880s were manifold. His writings and speeches were many and sometimes contradictory. Within all this, one issue which has stimulated debate among his biographers is: when did he become a socialist and what kind of socialist? Another issue is: what happened to his Christianity?

Fred Reid argues that Hardie was converted to socialism in 1887 but adds that he "had to pursue his vision cautiously, even deviously, in the Scottish situation where there were as yet few socialists who were not extremists".[14] William Stewart and Emrys Hughes, both of whom knew Hardie, date it a year later. In an article in *The Miner* in September 1888 Hardie attacked unshackled capitalism and declared: "The only possible remedy is a new economic departure in which our entire industrial society shall be worked on the principle of one vast co-operative. This would mean the advent of economic socialism, which is demanded alike by reason and equity." Not least, David Lowe quotes a letter (written in 1897) to him from Hardie in which he wrote: "In 1888 I saw that Socialism and independent action was the only hope of the worker."[15]

Clearly 1888–89 were crucial years in Hardie becoming a socialist. But what kind of socialist? Not the kind which wanted a violent revolution with the physical overthrow of rulers and their replacement by an unelected junta of workers. Despite his friendship with Engels in the late 1880s, he was not a Marxist. He was ready for class conflict but not class warfare.

Hardie was an egalitarian who believed that workers could achieve a social revolution by democracy. A new tax system could transfer money from the rich to the poor. He was a collectivist who wanted the state to run essential industries. Instead of being organized for private profit, they would serve the people. He was not saying that every corner shop should be swallowed by the state. He was not saying that no one should own their own house – after all, he did. He was saying that industries which, for instance, produced fuel or organized transport, and which were powerful enough to affect the lives of thousands of people, should be in public ownership. He believed that these socially run industries would facilitate fraternity, that is people in mutual relationships in which they cared for and valued each other. Later in 1896, addressing a huge open-air rally, he explained, "Socialism is not a system of economics… Those who doubt this would be asserting to the proposition that the highest form of inspiration was the multiplication table. I am a socialist because socialism means fraternity founded on justice, and the fact that in order to secure this it is necessary to transfer land and capital from private to public ownership."

STILL A CHRISTIAN

During this period, Hardie does not appear to have been a regular church-goer, although the records are scanty. But his Christian faith remained. In his book on Hardie, Morgan does not dwell on his religion. Nonetheless, writing of this period he says, "It was the religious conversion of 1878 rather than the industrial conversion of 1887 that remained the dominant experience of life to date."[16] Hardie himself declared that socialism was "a handmaiden of religion and as such entitled to the support of all who pray for the coming of Christ on Earth".

Hardie continued to look to the Gospels as his inspiration, even if their content was ignored by many Christians. He wrote in *The Miner*, "The world today is sick and weary at heart. Even our clergy are for the most part dumb dogs who dare not bark. So it was in the days of Christ. Those who proclaimed a God-given gospel to the world were the poor and the comparatively unlettered. We need today a return to the principles of that gospel which, by proclaiming all men sons of God and brethren one with another, makes it impossible for one, Shylock-like, to insist on his rights at the expense of another."

His reliance on Christ was seen in his strongly held views against violence. He pointed out that Jesus never used force, never wielded a sword, never backed a war as he extended his kingdom. It was seen in Hardie's attitude to money. The Gospels are full of Jesus' warnings about loving Mammon. Hardie rejected offers that would have given him financial security and social status. As Benn says, short of cash during the Mid Lanark by-election, he "behaved as he always did as if the Lord would provide".[17]

Not least, his faith seemed to bear him up in times of grief, as when his beloved daughter died, and times of defeat. After his failure at Mid Lanark, he wrote, in a defiant manifesto to those who voted for him: "The meaningless drivel of the ordinary politician must now give place to the burning words of earnest men, whose hearts are on fire with love to their kind, men who believe in the Fatherhood of God, the brotherhood of man."

The years 1887–88 were significant for Hardie. He established *The Miner*, which gave him a voice among miners and others. At some stage he embraced socialism – but not Marxism. He realized that the interests of the working class could not be advanced much by the Liberal Party and they needed their own party. He failed to win many votes at the Mid Lanark by-election but he stood as an independent candidate and went on to participate in the formation of the SLP. He had parted company with the Liberals for good and set up an alternative. His biggest disappointment must have been his failure to draw many trade unions into the Labour camp. Indeed, at the TUC conferences he faced bitter hostility from Lib–Lab MPs.

He visited London, met MPs, saw the House of Commons. He appeared to come to two decisions. One was that he should immerse himself in national politics rather than just trade union matters. The other was that he should spend more time in London, which was the political powerhouse of Britain.

CHAPTER 4

KEIR HARDIE MP, 1889–95

In the late 1880s Hardie developed an interest in political and social conditions abroad. He wrote about trade and industry in France and the USA. In 1888 he attended the International Trades Congress in London. More importantly, in July 1889 he went to the second Socialist International in Paris, where he represented both the Ayrshire miners and Scottish Labour. Other British delegates included Cunninghame Graham and William Morris, the artist and craftsman, who represented the Socialist League. At one point, Hardie declared that "no person in England believed in other than peaceful methods to achieve amelioration of condition". His statement angered Morris and the German Social Democrat delegates, who emphasized the need for revolution by force if necessary.

Hardie took the international meetings seriously and made friendships with several European Labour leaders. His readiness to listen and discuss, and his growing sense of statesmanship, won him respect from those who often disagreed with him. He was probably held in more respect in Europe than he was in

Britain. As a trade union leader, Hardie had been very critical, perhaps racist, toward Lithuanians and Poles who were brought into the mines to break strikes. He now acknowledged that they too were the victims of capitalism. His growing belief that real change could only come about by politics was also strengthened.

He started a new journal, the *Labour Leader,* to succeed *The Miner.* The first copy was headed by a poem by Alfred, Lord Tennyson about "The Christ that is to be" but it was not a religious paper. Nor was it a mining one. Its content, most of which was written by Hardie, reflected his larger political concerns. For instance, in April 1889 he argued that despite the Liberals' insistence on minimal state interference, the state was very active in protecting the wealthy and he called for the state to protect workers to enable them to enjoy "the whole of the wealth produced by them". He followed this on more familiar ground when he called for Lib–Lab MPs such as Henry Broadhurst and Charles Fenwick to be replaced by workers who would speak for workers. Perhaps Hardie was thinking of himself.

Hardie took every opportunity to attack Broadhurst. At the Trade Union Congress (TUC) in Dundee, he did it again and was met by a fierce counter attack, with Broadhurst sneering at him as "the great sage of Ayrshire". Hardie did not receive much support from the skilled workers who made up most of the congress but their dominance was about to be challenged. In 1880, only 381,000 workers were in trade unions. They were called "the labour aristocracy", as they tended to have had more training, to receive higher wages, and to possess greater job security than unskilled workers outside the trade union movement. They happily gave their support to the Lib–Lab MPs.

In 1888 in east London, match girls organized themselves, went on a strike against Bryant & May for better wages and safer work conditions, and won a famous victory. It was followed the next year by a successful strike by gas workers, led by Will Thorne, and the London dock strike, which won enormous public interest under Ben Tillett. Other strikes followed by bricklayers, firemen, boot-makers, and others. They were called the new unionism because their collective action was mainly by unskilled workers. The upsurge occurred because of a period of high employment, which meant that more unskilled people were in jobs and ready to be unionized. The improved basic education of working-class people might have meant that more could participate in the task of organizing. Almost certainly, the involvement of socialists was important. The gas and dock strikes were helped by Tom Mann and John Burns, both members of the Amalgamated Society of Engineers, and both charismatic, almost evangelical, socialists.

To revert to the Dundee congress: Hardie once again lost his proposal that the TUC promote an eight-hour day, but by a smaller margin than previously. Workers from London's new unions had backed him. Before long, Broadhurst resigned on grounds of ill health. To be sure, when the economy took a dip the new unions lost members. Nonetheless, they were to change the nature of the TUC, while some of their leaders, especially Will Thorne, made their voices heard.

The new unionism, then, was important as an emerging challenge to "the labour aristocracy". It was also to draw Hardie into the place where he would become an MP. He had been visiting London more often. Cunninghame Graham had taken him to see the House of Commons. At that time he met Frank Smith, a former Salvation Army officer who had left after disputes with General Booth over what Smith saw as its ineffective efforts to tackle poverty. He was a Christian socialist and he and Hardie took to each other. Thereafter Smith helped him in all his campaigns and sometimes acted as his personal and unpaid secretary. Kenneth Morgan says he was "perhaps the person closest to him and most attuned to his changing moods for the rest of his life".[1] Smith showed him around London.

STANDING FOR WEST HAM SOUTH

Cunninghame Graham had been actively involved in the London strikes and got Hardie to join him. Hardie's work in Scotland, his writings, and his stand at the TUC congresses had already made him known among socialists and radicals in east London. Now his presence, his experience, and his speaking ability were welcomed. Some socialists in the constituency of West Ham South, including Will Thorne, approached him about standing as their parliamentary candidate. Hardie was keen and, in order to give time to his prospects, resigned his post with the Ayrshire Miners' Union. The miners gave a dinner in Cumnock for him and Lillie, a brooch to Lillie, and money to Hardie, some of which came from mill girls whom he had helped to form a union. Now Hardie had no income and he handed the money to Lillie to open an account with the Ayrshire Building Society.

West Ham South had a Tory MP. Two Liberals wanted to be the challenger. One withdrew, leaving Hume Webster, a rich manufacturer, as the probable candidate. Hardie had agreed to stand for Labour and then a tragedy occurred that was also a stroke of luck for Hardie. In January 1892 Hume Webster committed suicide for reasons which are still not known. The Liberals were in such disarray that they never found a replacement and numbers indicated that they would back Hardie.

His position was unusually strong. Nonconformist clergy, who shared his temperance views, voiced their support. A local newspaper, the *West Ham Herald*, which was also pro temperance, backed him in print. Socialists and Labourites had made much progress in local elections to the council, the school board, and the board of guardians. Among the councillors was Will Thorne. Hardie's known advocacy of the eight-hour day appealed to many workers in West Ham. His more recent calls for a graduated income tax on all incomes over £1,000 a year, with the revenue to be spent on old-age pensions, was welcomed by those for whom old age often meant the workhouse. He cleverly gave attention to unemployment, which many in the constituency had experienced or feared. Indeed, it was to be a major theme for the rest of his life.

Hardie campaigned vigorously. He would speak in the open air at the dock gates at 5.30 a.m. and every day saw him proclaiming his case at numerous meetings. His eloquence in the open air was revealed in a report of one of his speeches in the *Workman's Times*. It recorded:

> Dealing with the criticism that he was not a local man, but a Scotsman, he replied, he was a Scotsman. Most of them were either Irishmen or Scotsmen but they were all labourers (Hear, hear). Their cause was the same and local circumstances sunk into insignificance before the magnitude and grandeur of the labour battle in which they were engaged and so much interested (Cheers). If they did return him it would prove that there was one part of the country where the labour question had taken root and was understood by the workers. What were the cries of the parties compared to their cry? The cry of the toiling millions, the cry of the 1,200 miners done to death every year in the bowels of the earth simply for lack of proper legislation. Men who went to sea in ships sometimes never came back again. How many lives would be saved if parliament were based on proper lines, and the representatives were honest working men instead of capitalists, as they now were?

Moved by his words, working-class men queued at his campaign rooms to be volunteer canvassers.

In his election address, Hardie wrote that he was standing

at the invitation of the United Liberal, Radical, and Labour Party of West Ham South as a Labour, Radical, and Home Rule candidate. He stated that he was in favour of nationalizing land, mines, banks, railways, docks, waterways, and tramways. He continued, "I have all my life given an independent support to the Liberal Party, but my first concern is the moral and material well-being of the working-classes, and, if returned, I will in every case place the claims of labour above those of party. Generally speaking, I am in agreement with the present programme of the Liberal Party so far as it goes, but I reserve to myself the absolute and unconditional right to take such action, irrespective of the exigencies of party welfare, as may to me seem needful in the interests of the workers." It must be added that Hardie might have approved of the Liberals' programme but they certainly would not agree with his calls for nationalization of many industries and services.

Major Banes, the sitting MP, had rarely spoken in the Commons and was not in much evidence in West Ham. On 4 July 1892 the result of the contest between what the press called the miner and the major was announced. It was a convincing win for the former. Hardie secured 5,268 votes and Banes 4,036. At the age of thirty-six, the one-time pit boy was an MP. The reason for his victory was, as Fred Reid wrote: "He had successfully linked trade unions, radicals and socialists in one coalition."[2] He might have added that the coalition also embraced many Christians.

Two other Labour candidates also won seats in the Commons: John Burns in Battersea and Havelock Wilson, founder of the National Sailors' and Firemen's Union, in Middlesbrough.

There followed the famous entry of Hardie into the House of Commons on 3 August. To his surprise, his supporters had hired a wagonette to take him. In it a lone trumpeter played the Marseillaise. At Parliament Square, Hardie got out and went into the Commons to the cheers of his backers. The press and his enemies reported falsely that Hardie had himself hired the transport, that a brass band marched with him, and that his rabble forced their way into Parliament.

He wore a plain tweed suit and a hat variously described as a workman's cap and a blue scotch cap, among others. Today it would be called a deer stalker. It was the hat which he displayed in the photo in his election leaflet. His suit was not the clothes worn in a mine or factory. It was a tweed suit of the kind worn by working-class men when, for instance, attending a meeting.

His dress caused an outburst against him. Most MPs wore a black frock coat, starched wing collars and black silk top hats. The Lib–Lab members conformed. John Burns arrived in such an outfit. The press attacked Hardie for being different and lowering standards. And not just the press: in September, T. R. Threlfall of the TUC – with whom Hardie had crossed swords before – spoke at a meeting of the Trades Congress in Edinburgh. A report exists in the Cumnock archives. Threlfall said of trade union men in the Commons that "if they had done nothing else they had demonstrated that working men could come like gentlemen". He continued that Mr Hardie "has outraged the sentiment of Labour and that he did serious injury to his own reputation by going to the House of Commons dressed in the manner he did", because "the House of Commons is the first assembly of gentlemen in the world". Uproar followed and the meeting was abandoned.

Hardie knew what he was doing. In 1887 he wrote in a local paper, "A local man in Parliament to do any good at all should be paid the current wages for the district he represents and for the trade he has been accustomed to work in. He should go to the House of Commons in workaday clothes." He appears to have planned his possible entrance to Parliament well beforehand.

A few weeks after his election but before he entered the

Commons, in July 1892, he spoke at a meeting in Dreghorn, in Scotland, which was reported by the *Kilmarnock Standard*. Hardie had said that in the House of Commons "he had no intention whatever of aping the manner and methods of the classes which were socially above him. He had been returned by working men as a Labour member and he intended to go to the House of Commons in that capacity." Hardie's mode of dress was quite deliberate. It was to show that he represented the working class.

Life as an MP

Being an MP in London posed two difficulties for Hardie. One was how he was to support himself and his family financially at a time when MPs received no salary. The other was that he would be spending even longer periods away from his wife and children.

He had refused money from the Liberals offered in return for being a tame Lib–Lab MP. No doubt Cunninghame Graham would have given him financial backing but he did not want that. He received numerous invitations to address meetings and he appeared to accept most, if not all, as a source of income. He charged an average of three guineas to cover travelling costs plus a fee for himself. In addition, he made some money from writing articles and just about coped.

The Hardies had lived in inadequate and overcrowded accommodation in Barrhill Road. Caroline Benn explains that "offers of money to Hardie were to be a feature for the rest of his life. Most came with strings attached and Hardie recognised this. Some givers may have hoped to head off extremism by making likely labour leaders dependants (a role corporate foundations and government agencies still seek to play); others were industrialists who had made it big and were into philanthropy, believing the world would be a safer place if the working class was tied to benefactors rather than led astray by revolutionaries."[3] Then he received an approach he was prepared to accept. In 1891 Adam Birkmyre, who had taken over Robert Owen's New Lanark mills and was dedicated to socialism, offered Hardie money to build a house. He refused the gift but agreed to take the money as an interest-free loan of £600. It was a mortgage which he paid off each year until he was free of debt. Keir and Lillie chose a site in Cumnock which slopes down to the River Lugar. Half villa, half cottage, it was named Lochnorris and still stands today.

Lillie was delighted with Lochnorris, although it meant keeping a bigger house and feeding and clothing the family on the £1 a week which her husband sent her. She was domestically hard-working, thrifty, and frugal. When Hardie was home he took a keen interest in the garden and they grew their own vegetables and fruit. She was not a great socializer and must have felt lonely and would have wished that her husband was there more with the children. But he was always glad to get home and liked nothing better than to be there with his family and had a particularly close relationship with his daughter, known as Nan.

The Cumnock archives contain a cutting from a local paper, possibly the *Cumnock Chronicle*, in which a reporter describes a visit to Lochnorris in September 1892. He wrote that a kindly, homely woman (Lillie) answered his knock and showed him in "with some words of hearty welcome". He saw Hardie in his small room known as his den, where there was not "a single item of luxury in his plainly furnished study". The reporter commented, as others did, "He looks much older than he is; but his eyes are peculiarly expressive, and there is something in his quiet manner which at once impresses you with his evident sincerity and thoroughgoing earnestness." He added how very fond Hardie was of his home and garden.

"MEMBER FOR THE UNEMPLOYED"

Back in Parliament, Hardie sat on the opposition benches, where he was joined initially by Burns and Wilson. The Liberal government, led by Gladstone for the fourth time, was preoccupied with the question of home rule for Ireland and it was not until 7 February 1893 that Hardie could make his maiden speech, which focused on the unemployed. He estimated that they numbered four million and graphically described their sufferings and that of their families. Unable to pay the rent, some were evicted from their homes, children went hungry, and numbers had to enter the workhouse. Pending more fundamental reforms to tackle unemployment, Hardie listed short-term measures, including an increase in government jobs in dockyards, factories, and arsenals, a proper minimum wage for labourers, a forty-eight-hour week for government employees (to make room for other workers), and possible experiments in land colonies, where men could live and work in farming occupations.

For once the press gave sympathetic coverage to Hardie. A report in the radical *Workman's Times* described the scene.

The House was quite full, and as Keir Hardie, with quiet deliberation, rose to his feet, honourable members settled themselves in their places with an air of assumed unconcern, as being unwilling to exhibit any vulgar curiosity as to what this man of the people might have to say now that he was among them... As Hardie passed from point to point in his temperate, intelligent statement of the claims of the common people, the House appeared to realise in some measure the phenomenon that had come along in a cap and a scarf and in an ill-fitting pair of trousers. For the first time the governors of the people, who have governed so long for their own profit, are come face to face with one of the people whom they have governed... Perhaps the most amusing feature of the incident was the change which gradually stole over the two front benches as Hardie unfolded his message to the House. The occupants of these benches at the outset had disposed themselves in the customary variety of attitudes prepared to lend, as it were, half an ear to the new member, and were stirred with just the faintest curiosity and a slightly supercilious curiosity at that, to hear what was coming... As Hardie developed his points, these two usually impassive front benches visibly stirred. By the time Hardie got through they were all eyes and ears.

Hardie did not win their support but he had made his mark and henceforth was known as "the member for the unemployed".

Soon he became an adept questioner of government ministers, particularly of the president of the local government board, as he urged the government to ensure that local authorities did more for those out of work. He was one of the very few MPs to protest when troops fired and killed two miners during a strike at Featherstone, Yorkshire. The Liberals took little action, which confirmed Hardie in his view that they were "the foe" of the workers.

It was not just unemployment and strikes. Hardie increasingly expressed his anger over the extent and nature of poverty. He accused the government of ignoring the plight of 20,000 women within a mile radius of St Paul's Cathedral who were working for 3s. 6d. a week (with some pushed into prostitution) and of children living rough. In June 1893 he took up the issue of the government dismissing workmen in its factories once they reached the age of forty-five. In one case, a man committed suicide and, on visiting his home, Hardie found his body still there as his wife could not afford to have him buried. Few MPs shared his anger.

No MP harried the government as much. When a dock strike broke out in Hull in which magistrates and troops clearly backed the shipowners, Hardie put a series of questions which continued for five weeks. He asked by whose authority army and navy forces were sent to Hull. Was the government aware that troops were loading and unloading ships? His questions forced the government to reveal that, of the thirty-nine magistrates, nineteen were shareholders in ships and four were shipowners. None were working men. Never before had a strike taken up so much of the time of Parliament.

In the Commons, he even asked questions about the wages and work conditions of those employed in Parliament such as messengers, waiters, and doormen. He was probably the first MP ever to do so.

Critics asserted that his one-man show in the Commons was ineffective. His call for more state action annoyed some Liberals and radicals who had voted for him in West Ham only to find that their MP was a wild socialist.

But his lone stand was significant for three reasons. First, he succeeded in raising the neglected evil of unemployment to public attention. This was important in itself but it also won the approval of the new unions, whose members were vulnerable to losing their jobs,

Second, by attempting to raise the wages of government employees, such as those who worked in prisons and arsenals, and local authority staff, he hoped to set standards which private employers would follow.

Third, he stuck to his strategy of forming an independent Labour Party, even if it had only one parliamentary member as Burns and Wilson moved toward the Liberals. Hardie was ready to vote for Liberal policies of which he approved, such as home rule, but he refused to take the Liberal whip. His determination was reinforced when in 1894 Gladstone, whom he admired, was replaced by Lord Rosebery, whom he did not.

Another criticism was that Hardie was often absent from the Commons. The criticism ignores the fact that he attended far more frequently than many richer members, who treated it like a club. None of them, like Hardie, spent day after day, week after week, questioning government ministers. Nonetheless it is true that he spent longish periods away. It is true that he often found Parliament boring and snobbish. More to the point, he believed that he could contribute to building the Labour cause outside Parliament. He never ceased campaigning. The *Labour Leader* showed that, at this time, he spent one week as follows: Tuesday, open-air meetings in West Ham; Wednesday, in the Commons; Thursday, office work before catching the overnight train to Scotland; Friday, socialist agitation in Scotland; Saturday, spoke to a Labour demonstration in Dundee and then caught the overnight train to Leeds; Sunday, speeches at Leeds, Keighley, and Halifax; Monday, speeches at Halifax, Bradford, and Bolton.

In August 1894, a fiery talk he gave to 2,000 striking Ayrshire miners in Kilmarnock was reported by the *Kilmarnock Chronicle*. Hardie said: "There was something inspiring in the spectacle of what was practically a nation within a nation, fighting as one man to ensure what they believed to be their own." He continued that MPs "read in the papers of women and children starving. Had these been the wives and children of princes, aristocrats and landlords would parliament then say they could do nothing to relieve this suffering and this hunger? No; all the powers of the state would have been set in motion to provide a huge out-door relief fund for these royal and aristocratic paupers (laughter) and what parliament would have done for them, he demanded, should be done for the men and women, the children of the common people (applause)."

Hardie perceived that more people could be reached by the printed word than by the spoken word. In March 1894 he converted the *Labour Leader* into an enlarged weekly. Its base in Glasgow was extended by one in Fleet Street, London. The latter sounded grand but was a dilapidated office with weak floor boards of which Hardie cheerily warned supporters, "If you are under 17 stone, call the first day you are in London." Hardie was the overall editor, with the talented David Lowe in charge of the Scottish edition. It soon had a readership of 50,000.

Hardie owned the paper. He appointed the staff and contributors, some of whom were his Christian socialist friends. Lily Pearce wrote a column, Hardie wrote the children's section. Mary McPherson, a rare woman graduate, was often in Paris with her husband and covered the international scene. One helper was Keir's youngest brother, George, whom David Lowe described: "Sunny, active, hopeful, his presence in the offices in those grey days was valuable."[4] Years later, after Keir's death, George also became a Labour MP. Others came in to lend a hand with the paper. They were a committed group and the Scottish office often held parties to which their families were invited. The supposedly dour Hardie would dance and sing Scottish songs.

With a wage bill of £750 a year plus printing expenses, finance was a problem. Hardie received donations from Christian socialist friends, particularly Bream Pearce, husband of Lily Pearce. When things got really desperate, Hardie dug into his own resources: on one occasion he sold his treasured and complete set of Carlyle's books and on another he mortgaged his small life insurance policy. Happily by 1896 the paper was just about paying its way. Robert Blatchford, a successful journalist, humanist, and socialist, started *The Clarion* in 1891. Probably it was not as earnest as the *Labour Leader* and gave more coverage to sport and the theatre. Hardie and Blatchford were never good friends and now became rival editors. But both papers had wide readerships and, at a time when a number of political papers had short lives, these two survived.

Hardie's control of the *Labour Leader* came in for the understandable criticism that it was owned by Hardie himself, not a collective of Labour supporters. On the other hand it was Hardie who raised the cash and whose drive made it successful. Morgan – who had his criticisms of Hardie – concluded: "For thousands of working people and for radical middle-class sympathisers, it became the most influential vehicle for their discontent with social conditions."[5]

INDEPENDENT LABOUR PARTY

Labour now had a paper and an MP but not, except in Scotland, a party. Joseph Burgess, who had supported Hardie's election campaign in West Ham, had other ideas. He was well known as a strong socialist in Yorkshire and was also prominent in the Bradford and District Labour Union, which had grown in working-class numbers following outrage at the tactics of Liberal factory-owners during a strike. He was editor of the short-lived *Workman's Times* and it was within its pages that he proposed that local labour groups and individuals form a national Labour Party. Hardie co-operated with him and, when plans were made for a national conference at Bradford, a hive of labour and socialist activity, he spread the news at his many speaking engagements.

The conference in January 1893 was attended by over 120 delegates, including Bruce Glasier, Robert Smillie, Ben Tillett, Cunninghame Graham, Robert Blatchford, Bernard Shaw, Joseph Burgess, and Pete Curran of the Gas Workers. Henry Pelling adds that, as well as these old hands, "The most interesting feature of the gathering was the presence of a new type of political delegate – the intelligent, respectable, working trade unionist of the new labour clubs... they were the working class in earnest, the product of the new education and the widening franchise."[6] He added that their enthusiasm and discipline impressed the press, who had been attracted by the phenomenon of working-class people organizing a national body without middle-class oversight.

Emrys Hughes recalls that, twenty-one years later, Hardie could list twenty-six of those present and had written: "Every little incident in the proceedings stands out clearly in my memory." He added that he had attended the conference "fully determined not to accept office of any kind. Even then I had learnt that nature had not intended me to be a boss."[7] But after the chair of the conference proved incapable, Hardie was elected to take over and fulfilled the role brilliantly. He was, as Morgan put it, the conference's "dominant personality, showing how the impact of his entry into parliament had permeated far beyond West Ham".[8]

The formation of the new party was never in doubt. The debates were about its title, objective and programme. Some wanted it called the Socialist Labour Party. Katherine St John Conway, a teacher and socialist from Bristol, who later married Bruce Glasier, rose to oppose. She argued that having socialist in the name would limit recruitment. Ben Tillett agreed, saying that many trade unionists were socialists at work every day but associated socialism with violent revolution. Hardie rejoiced, for he knew that a national party had to possess a broad gate which accepted labourites, Liberals disillusioned with the Liberal Party, and socialists. The conference agreed on the name of the Independent Labour Party (ILP).

Pelling comments on the importance of this decision, which "reflected an awareness of the origins and roots of the party in the local labour unions and parties, some of which were not explicitly committed to socialism... the theoretical approach gives way to the practical".[9] The decision about the name did not mean that the new party did not wish to move towards socialism. Its objective, carried by a large majority, was "to secure the collective ownership of the means of production, distribution and exchange".

The party's programme, drawn up by a sub-group and

amended by the full conference, included the eight-hour working day, the prohibition of the employment of children under fourteen, provision for the sick, disabled, aged, widows, and orphans, and free primary, secondary, and university education. Two fiscal reforms were the abolition of indirect taxation and a graduated income tax. Hardie's influence was seen in proposals to limit the consumption of alcohol. Not least, the conference decided: "The Independent Labour Party is in favour of every proposal for extending electoral rights and democratising the system of government."

It was agreed that affiliation was the basis of membership so that a wide range of bodies (and their members), such as trade unions, trade councils, labour clubs, labour churches, and socialist groups, could be embraced within the ILP. Membership was open to women, unlike other parties which had separate women's committees. Also unlike other parties, women could be elected to the executive. Hardie heartily approved. His support for women's rights was of long standing and did not coincide with the later rise of the suffragette movement.

Lastly, there was the issue of the executive or National Administrative Council (NAC). Initially it was formed on a regional basis with fifteen members. It proved unwieldy and at the second ILP conference in 1894 the regionalism was dropped and the membership reduced to nine. At this time, Hardie, despite his determination to stay out of office, was elected as party chair (initially called president) and remained so for a long period.

Morgan declares that the outcome of the conference shows "the political genius of Hardie".[10] As Iain McLean put it: "The delegates steered a careful path between the Scylla of Lib–Labbery and the Charybdis of sectarianism."[11] A party independent of the Liberals and Tories had been formed which would offer an alternative programme to the electorate. It was flexible enough to draw in labourites who were not socialists.

Simultaneously, socialists would join because the promotion of socialism was implicit in its objective.

At the close of the conference, Hardie insisted on the singing of 'Auld Lang Syne'. There was a feeling of fellowship, almost religion, with the delegates becoming disciples who would evangelize Britain politically.

The ILP had major weaknesses. It lacked cash and did not even have an office. The bulk of the delegates came from the West Riding, Lancashire, and Scotland. Mining districts such as South Wales, Northumberland, and Durham were under-represented. Few came from the south of England, not even from London. The new unions were often in London but their membership and effectiveness fluctuated with employment and unemployment. The north tended to have long-serving employees in cotton and woollen factories who were able to give stable support to the ILP. Initially it was almost a provincial party.

Nonetheless, an independent party had been founded. Soon afterwards, in March 1893, Hardie explained its importance. Liberal reforms had been insufficient. The people

are free to hold any or no religious beliefs; they are free to vote or abstain from voting... They are not free to live the lives which they feel stirring within. The means of existence are owned by others, and are used to add to the wealth of the nation at the expense of the life of the people. The ILP is the outcome of all this... Its members look on the untilled land and the unemployed and ask, why are these complements not brought together? They see their aged poor suffering the indignities of our inhuman Poor Laws and themselves hurrying on to a like fate, and Liberalism has no word of hope or cheer... The aim of the ILP is to create a genuinely Independent Party in politics to take charge of the revolution which economic conditions are leading us toward; and its objective is to build up an industrial commonwealth in which none will suffer want because of the over-abundance of others.

Hardie was saying again that Liberal reforms did not change the economic conditions which pauperized people. Only the new party would do this. The ILP was the forerunner of the Labour Party which eventually won general elections. Numerous people contributed to the formation of the ILP but Hardie was the foremost.

ATTACKS ON THE ROYAL FAMILY

The year 1894 was to be Hardie's last full year as MP for West Ham South. Bruce Glasier said that Hardie "never felt at home in parliament", but "its importance, however, as a national rostrum overbore his misgivings".[12] In the Commons, he was certainly on a national rostrum when he attacked the royal family. Already in 1893 he had tried to move a motion which deplored the House's congratulations to the Duke of York on his marriage. This was just brushed aside by the members. His persistent attacks the following year were treated much more seriously and earned him a volume of abuse from press and Parliament.

His political fuse was the disaster at Albion Colliery at Cilfnydd in South Wales on 23 June 1894, which killed over 250 men and boys. On the same day, the Duchess of York gave birth to a son. The next day President Carnot was assassinated in France. A few days later, Hardie had an outraged article in the *Labour Leader*: "Two hundred and fifty human beings, full of strong life in the morning, reduced to charred and blackened heaps of clay in the evening. The air rent with the wail of the childless mother, the widowed wife, and the orphaned child... Only those who have witnessed such scenes, as I have twice over, can realize what they mean... Coal must be cheap even if 1200 sturdy miners are murdered yearly in the process – 1200 hearths made desolate."

His anger at the deaths of his fellow miners was multiplied

by the fact that the Commons and the press virtually ignored the disaster, while giving prominence to the birth of a child and the assassination of one man. His article continued that "everyone would mourn with Madame Carnot, and rejoice in a subdued kind of way with the Duke and Duchess of York in the birth of their child, but it is to the sore-stricken poor of the Welsh valley that the true hearts of this great nation will turn with its overwelling sympathy... The life of one Welsh miner is of greater commercial and moral value to the British nation than the whole Royal Crowd put together, from the Royal Great Grand-mama down to this puling Royal Great Grand-child."

What he wrote in his article, Hardie was not afraid to repeat in Parliament. A vote of condolence with the French people was moved in the Commons and Hardie asked if it could be extended to the bereaved in South Wales. He was brushed aside and when the government moved congratulations to the Duke and Duchess of York, Hardie was on his feet: "Mr Speaker, on my behalf and those whom I represent I am unable to join in this public address. I owe no allegiance to any hereditary ruler." Two senior MPs tried to get him overruled but Hardie would not stop. "I was about to observe that I know nothing in the career of the Prince of Wales which commends him especially to me... Sometimes we get glimpses of the Prince at the gaming tables, sometimes on the racecourse. His Royal Highness is Duke of Cornwall, and as such he draws £60,000 from the Duchy property in London, which is made up of some of the vilest slums."

The speaker ordered Hardie to keep to the motion, so he went on: "From his childhood onward this boy will be surrounded by sycophants and flatterers by the score and will be taught to believe himself as of a superior creation... I protest against this motion being passed, and if there is another member of the House who shares the principles I hold I will carry my protest the length of a division. The government will not find an opportunity for a vote of condolence with the relatives of those who are lying stiff and stark in a Welsh valley."

His determined and fiery speech was made amid shouting and catcalling. One reporter described the scene in the Commons: "I've been in a wild beast show at feeding time. I've been at a football match when the referee gave a wrong decision... but in all my natural life I've never witnessed a scene like this. They howled and yelled and screamed but he stood his ground." There was no other member willing to support him. The popular press turned on Hardie with abuse. Both MPs and the press accused him of being hostile to the monarchy, wanting to destroy the establishment, and being opposed to the will of the people. He became a hate figure. Yet he had his admirers and received so many letters in support of his actions that he had to hire two men to open them. The ILP, in general, rejoiced that their leader was standing up to the royal family. Later he protested when a former speaker, Lord Peel, was granted a pension of £400 when, as Hardie put it, "the House of Commons seemed not to have the time nor the inclination to provide a system of pensions for the aged workers of the country".

Morgan believes that Hardie's republicanism and attacks on the royal family were a grave mistake, given that Queen Victoria had become a popular monarch much admired by the bulk of the population. They strengthened the view that he was a political fanatic. Maybe, but his criticisms overlook the essentials that made Hardie tick. Hardie identified wholly with the working class and he was enraged that the deaths of these miners should be ignored. Further, he was a genuine democrat who saw no consistency in the Liberal practice of extending the franchise while allowing the head of state to be unelected.

Benn doubts if Hardie really was a republican and cites his words that the removal of the monarchy would have to wait for fundamental changes in economic and political conditions.

But this does not mean he backtracked on the republicanism he often asserted. As William Stewart, who knew him, put it: "He was certainly a republican, but like most socialists, he regarded the monarchy as simply an appanage of the political and social system, which would disappear as a matter of course when the system disappeared."[13] It was a matter of timing.

Whatever the pros and cons of Hardie's onslaught on the royal family, three points are clear. First, he displayed enormous courage. Not a single MP would stand with him. The major papers united in condemning him. He knew this would happen but it did not stop him. Second, as Benn explains, his attack sprang from "straight Old Testament rage against kings".[14] Third, his protests on behalf of South Wales miners and their families won him admiration in a country where – unknown to him – he was to fight a future election.

FAMILY LIFE

What with campaigning, the ILP, and the Commons, Hardie found it difficult to spend much time at home. He missed both his family and his house and garden. He realized that his absences imposed pressures on Lillie and he wrote almost every day – often by postcard.

In 1895 (or 1896), Hardie was offered money by two sisters, Elizabeth and Jean Kippen, who had received an inheritance from their father. They were supporters of home rule for Ireland and the common ownership of land in Scotland. They had also heard pleasing reports about Hardie but, before contacting him, they wanted to be sure that he was a good family man. They visited his mother-in-law, Sarah Wilson, then Lillie, and also asked questions about Hardie in Cumnock. They were satisfied and offered him £300 a year – a very substantial sum in those days – as long as he remained an MP and supported their two causes. Hardie talked it over with Lillie, who must have thought that her financial difficulties could be over. But eventually Hardie declined the offer on the grounds that he should not accept money which tied him to specific causes. He did say to the sisters that their kind offer would be best directed to organizations, for instance the Scottish Labour Party, rather than individuals. Lillie's attitude to the offer and her response to her husband's refusal of it is not known.

In early 1894, Hardie's daughter Nan had a period of illness. Hardie came home and must have been especially disturbed, having already suffered the loss of one daughter. The next year Lillie was ill. The nature of her sickness is not known: she could have been exhausted. She looked after three growing children (Jamie, Nan, and Duncan), the house and garden. She received regular visits from Hardie's two youngest brothers, David and George, and from Hardie's mother. She seemed to welcome and enjoy these but they would have meant extra demands on her time and purse. Once again, Hardie came home for a time.

What of the ILP during this period? Within a year it had 400 branches, mostly in Yorkshire, Lancashire, and Cheshire, with a total membership of 50,000 individuals. At its second conference in 1894, the talented Tom Mann, an engineer, was appointed secretary.

The Liberals, without Gladstone to hold them together, were disunited and the ILP did well at by-elections. Shortly after the formation of the party, it contested one at Halifax and took a quarter of the votes. It also won seats at local elections. It had no overall control of any local authority but its councillors pressed for improvements to the wages and work conditions of council employees – which won the approval of their trade union.

ILP members were also prominent in setting up relief centres and marching on demonstrations during times of high unemployment. The winter of 1894–95 was bitterly cold. In Lambeth, the Reverend F. B. Meyer, appalled by the suffering and lack of state help, declared, "These people must be relieved, and God will provide the wherewithal."[15] His teams, which included working-class residents, organized hot meals for children in the church and went out with food and blankets to adults. Across the river in West Ham, his fellow Christian Keir Hardie pushed the local authority to do more. His efforts were such that even the House of Commons took note and set up a select committee of twenty-five members to consider the distress caused by unemployment. Hardie was appointed to it, the first time an ILP MP was recognized in this way. Moreover, it occurred two years after Gladstone had refused to have such a committee because it was not the business of the government to deal with such matters. Hardie gave evidence and made proposals which were overruled. Then he had to stop attending when Lillie was ill and he went home. The committee petered out.

Another indication of the growing importance of the ILP was the calibre of some of its recruits. One was the 28-year-old Ramsay MacDonald. Like Hardie, MacDonald was the illegitimate son of a Scottish mother. Self-educated to a higher standard than Hardie, he held down administrative posts and supported the Liberal Party. He became angry at their refusal to appoint him as a candidate and threw in his lot with the ILP. As McLean observed, "Here was no Damascus road conversion. MacDonald joined the forces of labour out of cool, self-interested calculation and political analysis."[16] Nonetheless, the recruitment of such a talented young man showed the pulling power of the ILP. Moreover, he also brought his socialist wife, Margaret. As Margaret Gladstone she was the daughter of a Liberal professor with aristocratic connections. Her yearly allowance of £450 gave MacDonald the financial security lacked by most ILP politicians.

In 1895 a general election looked likely. Hardie recalls a visit to speak at Oxford University. Balliol College would not let him in but the less prestigious Manchester College did so.

Hardie commented that the future leaders of the nation were well versed in academic books but: "They will go out into the great world as unfitted for their task as if they were inhabitants who had suddenly been transplanted from another planet… Most of them will know as little of the real life and feelings of the common people as if they did not exist." It reinforced his belief that working-class people were required in Parliament. The ILP was ready, with twenty-eight candidates of whom Hardie had high hopes.

CHRISTIANITY AND SOCIALISM

Throughout these years, Christianity continued to be a feature of Hardie's talks, writings and life. The relationship between his faith and socialism became clearer. He did not adopt Darwinism; he did not follow the Liberal theologians who cast doubts on the divinity of Christ and on the divine inspiration of the Bible. His emphasis was on repeating the teaching of Jesus, that material greed was a barrier to the Christian's close walk with God. He said, "I think the millionaire is the worst case. He is ruined not only for time, but, if we are to believe the New Testament, for eternity."

His understanding of the practice of Jesus was that he lived among, befriended, and gave priority to the poor. His understanding of his teaching was that, as all people were equal in the sight of God, the earth's resources and goods should be shared fairly between them so that none suffered material want or social disadvantage. But it was not just about material fairness. He believed that more equal conditions created the environment in which fellowship (or fraternity) would flourish. In short, the objective was to promote right relationships between God and people and between people themselves.

By this time, there was no doubt that Hardie was a socialist

KEIR HARDIE MP, 1889–95

and a Christian; he sometimes called it Christian socialism. He saw socialism as a major means of establishing the kind of society God wanted. To be sure, he also increasingly recognized that Marxists based their socialism more on economic analysis and certain values – although the values were not Christian ones.

Hardie welcomed non-Christians into the ILP and the socialist movement. He had much sympathy for members of the SDF, although he could not accept their readiness to use violence, which he regarded as opposed to the teachings of Christ. Yet he reckoned that the non-religious socialists were participating in the promotion of the kingdom of God. He once stated: "I believe that democracy to be at bottom devoutly religious." It followed that when the non-Christians were pursuing such ends as democracy and equality, they were at one with the Christians. This was not to say that Christian socialists and non-Christian socialists were the same. It was to say there was a considerable overlap.

Hardie wanted to revive, not to repress, Christianity. In 1893 he addressed the congress of the Congregational Union of England and Wales and a report of his talk contained the following: "Christianity today lay buried, bound up in the cerements of a dead and lifeless theology. It awaited decent burial, and they in the Labour movement had come to resuscitate the Christianity of Christ, to go back to the time when the poor should have the gospel preached to them, and the gospel should be good news of joy and happiness in life." His words provoked such an uproar that he had to be shepherded away. In his view, in general the church, far from upholding the teachings of Christ, upheld the position of the rich. He frequently attacked it.

He rounded on the clergy who did not challenge a social economic system which meant wealth for some and poverty for others. Dr Storey, Moderator of the General Assembly of the Church of Scotland, had criticized paid agitators – by which he meant socialists – for upsetting people with their new doctrines. Hardie soon hit back in a talk which was reported as follows: "He (Mr Hardie) challenged him to state his stipend and whether or not he was a paid agitator who leads his congregation by the nose." He continued, "Perhaps the reverend gentleman will say what law it is that gives the Duke of Hamilton £114,000 a year in the shape of mineral royalties and allows each of the miners who dig the coal on which the royalty is paid £50 a year."

Again, he crossed swords with clergy who argued that religion should be kept out of politics. In an article in a journal, Hardie responded: "A late Bishop of the Church of England said that Christianity could not be applied to the affairs of Government. So much the worse, say I, for the nation. The code of ethics which cannot be applied to the aggregated life of the community we call the state should not be applied to the lives of the individuals who compose the state... I lay it down as a broad, unchallengeable Christian principle that any system of production or exchange which sanctions the exploitation of the weak by the strong or the unscrupulous is wrong and therefore sinful."

In 1894 Professor Flint, professor of divinity at Edinburgh University, delivered a public lecture in which he argued that socialism was basically anti-Christian because it allied itself with atheism and materialism; because it assumed that man's chief end on earth was a happy life rather than glorifying God; because it attached more importance to the condition of men rather than their character; and because it did injustice to the rights of individuals whose money and property could be taken from them.

Hardie replied in an article in which he started by saying that socialism allied itself only with socialism, not any other "ism". Socialism was not the same as anti-Christian Marxism.

He went on that man's chief end may be to glorify God but the economic and political systems upheld by people such as Flint hardly helped the masses so to do. "A man stunted in body, dwarfed in mind and sordid in spirit" could not glorify God. "A competitive and profit mongering system of industry... put it out of the reach of people."

He continued that socialism was about improving characters and it recognized that better circumstances and conditions made it easier for them to improve. Socialism might limit the so-called right of some individuals to accumulate profits. This is done to free the masses to develop their individuality. Hardie stated, "The primary rights of the individual are the right to work and the right to receive the full value of his labour." He ended with the biting comment that "the more a man knows about theology the less he is likely to know about Christianity". And much more. He argued that the practice of some churches of having superior pews for the rich and powerful reinforced sinful class divisions. He agreed with clerics who regretted the ill-treatment of Christians in other countries but asked why they did nothing about children starving to death in Britain.

Hardie's readiness to take on church heavyweights and the quality of his responses reveal that Christianity was of the utmost importance to him. He was not alone in his Christian position and he attracted Christians who shared his views and belonged to Christian socialist bodies. Frank Smith in London, Bream Pearce in Scotland, and Fred Jowett in Bradford are good examples. It should be added that there were clergymen and churches of all denominations who believed that Christianity had to be expressed in political action to create a more just society. In her study of evangelical social work, Kathleen Heasman shows that, by the end of the nineteenth century, even some from this conservative tradition "were often in favour of the modification of the class structure".[17] Stephen Mayor in his research found numbers of clergymen in various denominations who "were led to identify their causes and themselves with the Labour Party".[18] Nonetheless, they were a minority and Hardie chose to attack the overall impact of the churches, which was to uphold an unequal society.

In like manner, he was often critical of Christian charities. He came across one which claimed it was the cheapest charity because it could send a slum child into the country to be fed for 9d. In the *Labour Leader,* Hardie sarcastically wrote about how grateful the children must be to get away from poverty for one day. The charities should attempt to change society, not just one child for one day. He likened the concept of "the cheapest charity" to the cheapness of sub-standard goods sold to the poor. He ended: "The Christian world has got sadly astray. They do not know that they have forgotten the centre cross, and are worshipping at the cross of the thief."

At a meeting in the Kilmarnock Town Hall, Hardie responded to a talk by Mr Stephen Williamson MP, who was an employer and supporter of charities. A reporter recorded that Hardie immediately attacked Williamson, saying that to him "the duty of the Christian was to rob the worker and wound him more that he might show his Christian charity by pouring oil on his wounds and paying two pence for a bed for him at some hospitable inn. He (Hardie) had a very different idea of the conception of Christianity. The first duty of the Christian was to give to the worker his own and having done so they could dispense with the Christian charity."

Hardie did admire the Salvation Army and sometimes joined officers on their rounds when they found and fed the homeless. He once visited one of its homes for abandoned babies, where he was overcome by tears. General Booth, the founder of the Salvation Army, initially seemed to favour socialism but later criticized it. Hardie asked the reason why he had changed and then answered his own question: "One thing only. The Independent Labour Party has come and brought Socialism within measurable distance, and the rich supporters of General Booth have taken alarm." Nonetheless, he continued: "Whatever General Booth's failings may be, he has demonstrated his right to rank among the leaders of man. To him and his followers, Christianity is a reality. Whilst others have been praying to God to do something, General Booth had been doing it." And, of course, they agreed about the evils of drink.

SPIRITUALITY

In regard to his religion, it is also relevant to what people who knew or wrote about him called his "spirituality". Stewart describes an incident in 1892 when, after a conference in Norwich, Hardie and friends strolled into the grounds of the cathedral. They watched the sun set and the darkness rise. Suddenly the voice of Hardie was heard giving expression to the 23rd Psalm and soon the others, Christians and agnostics alike, joined in. They felt both at peace and at one with each other.

Stewart added, "This inherent spiritual emotionalism was continually manifesting itself in various ways all through his life... He was imbued with an imaginative catholicity of spirit which rendered him responsive to every expression of religious feeling which seemed to him sincere. His spiritual enthusiasm never led him out of touch with reality. In a very literal sense, 'the poor he always had with him'. He was one of them. And to him their cause was a cause of the devotional spirit."[19]

Two years later, a reporter from a serious journal watched Hardie and wrote, "Above all things a spiritual yet a simply practical man."

It is difficult to describe but, from his words and those of the people who knew him well, he comes across as a man who was immune to many worldly influences. He never pursued money, status, or popularity. He insisted on remaining close to working-class people even when all other so-called Labour MPs dressed and behaved like middle-class members. Poverty and suffering moved him to tears and anger. For the sake of the poor and unemployed, he was ready to take abuse, even hatred. Simultaneously, he loved nature, rivers, mountains, fields, animals. He would gladly spend much time in the crowded slums, yet he also loved to retreat to be alone in the hills. He was more than a politician. He was not just a Christian. The word "spiritual" does aptly describe him.

OUT OF THE COMMONS

Hardie's spirituality did not seem to help him in the 1895 general election which followed the disunited Liberal Party's defeat in the Commons. Despite their high hopes, not one of the ILP's twenty-eight candidates won a seat. In West Ham South, Major Banes employed a large number of men and had quietly made himself better known. The number of Labour councillors on the council had declined but Hardie still felt confident; probably over-confident, for he spent too much time in other ILP constituencies and not enough in his own. On the day, in a straight fight, Banes secured 4,750 votes and defeated Hardie with his 3,975. The Tories, moreover, returned to government.

Why did Hardie lose? A number of Liberals who had voted for him previously found his socialism too extreme and his willingness to co-operate with the Liberal Party too little. Nonconformists were disappointed that he gave less priority to temperance issues. Some Roman Catholic priests advised their flock against Hardie, saying that his plans for nationalizing land would endanger their schools and churches. Not least, as an MP Hardie had not given enough attention to his constituents, as he was frequently away campaigning or promoting the ILP.

Beatrice Webb of the Fabians, who had always looked down upon Hardie and his hopes for a working-class party, wrote with evident pleasure, "The ILP has completed its suicide," and predicted that Hardie would "sink into the old place of a discredited Labour leader". John Burns MP, a one-time socialist who was moving to the Liberal camp, rejoiced that the ILP's defeat was "the most costly funeral since Napoleon" and jeered that in Parliament Hardie had been "senseless, sentimental, anti-socialist and futile".[20] Some erstwhile supporters blamed Hardie for the defeats. Even MacDonald criticized him. With not a single MP, with funds exhausted by the election, the future of the ILP in general and Hardie in particular seemed bleak.

CHAPTER 5

Fight with Lord Overtoun; Friendship with the TUC, 1895–1900

The press blamed Hardie's lack of leadership and over-zealous socialism for the poor showing of the Independent Labour Party (ILP) in 1895. By contrast, the Social Democratic Federation (SDF) blamed his lack of socialism.

On examination, other than in Glasgow, the ILP's candidates performed with credit. The average vote per candidate was 1,500, which, in some places, cost Liberals their seats to the Tories – who won the general election. Hardie and Mann, as chair and secretary, had worked as hard as possible for their party and retained the backing of most members.

Some critics asked just what Hardie had achieved as an MP. Before entering the Commons he may have raised unrealistic hopes with his manifesto for nationalizing banks, railways, and docks. But, in reality, one MP could not bring about radical legislation. Caroline Benn has no doubt that his period in Parliament was worthwhile in that he raised the plight of those who had been ignored, particularly the unemployed and poor. She eloquently insisted that his contribution was "to insist that parliament honour all citizens equally and hear the innumerable small questions of working people's lives that mattered more to them than trade or treaties: degrading Poor Laws, low wages, unsafe working practices, long hours, ill health, charges for school, denial of rights to assemble, and the wanton use of police powers to 'discipline' citizens with grievances into silence".[1]

Whatever he had achieved, Hardie was downcast by the election results. He was subject to bouts of depression that almost turned to despair. Ethel Snowden, the wife of Philip Snowden, who joined the ILP at this time, wrote that socialist pioneers had to pay the price of "misunderstanding and abuse, cruel slanders and countless lies all along the road to Calvary and the cross at the end of it".[2] She knew Hardie as a fellow Christian socialist and had him in mind.

Certainly, he did sometimes regard himself as a martyr. Yet one of his great characteristics was that, if knocked down, he refused to be knocked out. Soon after the defeat, he was again writing with enthusiasm in the *Labour Leader*: "There is no need for despondency, much less despair… Thousands of our members are young men who have no votes. Most of these will be voters next time. I will be disappointed if in addition to these we have not also our women enfranchised by another election… Fight every by-election, fight the municipal elections as they come round, prepare for the grand struggle at the next election. A fighting party will make converts."

Tour of the USA

Whatever British voters thought of him, Hardie was increasingly well known in the English-speaking world. In September he left, accompanied by Frank Smith, for the USA. Once on board ship at Liverpool, he addressed his fellow travellers on the subject of "Competition" and illustrated the class system by pointing to the ship's division between those in steerage and those in upper-class saloons. As they drew closer to New York, he refused to change his watch to US time and retained Cumnock time so that he could always think of what his family were doing back home.

He had been invited by the American Labor Day Committee to speak at their conference in Chicago. Having successfully completed this appointment, he visited the American socialist Eugene Debs, in prison for his political activities. He then toured numerous towns, seeking out small groups of working-class activists, and urging them not just to strike but also to form a socialist movement.

In San Francisco the mayor offered him a bribe of $100,000 (£20,000) to push his economic interests in Britain. Hardie declined but could have done with some money soon after in Bute City, when Frank and himself were down to their last dollar. He recorded what happened next in some notes he jotted down: "A familiar sound came and set my blood tingling. It was the skirl of the bagpipes." They found a 6 foot 4 inch Scottish Highlander in national costume playing in a bar. He and his daughter then threw a party for them. Hardie concluded, "Nothing had been said about money but at the close when the cheering had died away… our Mac handed me seventy five dollars and that was how Providence came to our rescue at Bute City."

Back in Britain in December, Hardie soon faced a new year fraught with difficulties. A by-election took place in Aberdeen and the local ILP rejected Hardie as their candidate and chose the ILP's secretary, Tom Mann. Aberdeen was one of the strongholds of Henry Champion, a somewhat eccentric Tory socialist who supported the Social Democratic Federation.

Not surprisingly, Champion and Hardie did not get on and the former's influence probably explains why Tom Mann, friendly to the SDF, was selected. Hardie felt aggrieved but had to admit that Mann did well to win 2,479 votes.

In July 1896 Hardie must almost have despaired at the International Socialist Conference in London. Three of the five days were taken up debating whether anarchists should be admitted. On the last and fifth day, few turned up at 9.30 a.m. and the *Labour Leader* dryly commented (presumably in Hardie's words) that delegates prepared "to establish any number of proletarian armies to fight for the revolution were not prepared to get up in the morning for it". Hardie meanwhile spoke of the need for free comprehensive education without academic selection at any point. It was nearly a hundred years before his arguments were seriously taken up.

In October, Hardie did stand at a by-election in East Bradford. He was backed financially by the ILP's new treasurer, T. D. Benson, an accountant who also arranged a holiday for Lillie, who had been unwell, and the children. Hardie finished bottom of the poll, with the Liberals making much of his so-called revolutionary tendencies.

To be sure, it was not all gloom. In the summer of 1896, Manchester magistrates tried to stop ILP members speaking in the open air at a public arena at Boggart Hole Clough. Several were fined and two imprisoned. The ILP cleverly brought in Emmeline Pankhurst, whose husband was a local lawyer and member of the ILP, to speak. The magistrates were reluctant to imprison a woman and, while they dithered, Emmeline and Hardie addressed a huge crowd. Eventually the magistrates withdrew and the ILP claimed a victory for free speech.

The ILP also performed well at local elections and, before long, had 600 councillors. To Hardie's delight, Frank Smith eventually became a member of the London City Council. Nonetheless, the ILP's total membership was falling and

Hardie was making no progress in his wish to extend co-operation with trade unions and the Trade Union Congress (TUC). Indeed, miners' trade union leaders refused to share a platform with him at Durham, presumably because of Hardie's continuing attacks on their Lib–Lab MPs.

Given the lack of political progress, some ILP members, including Tom Mann, began to press for a socialist amalgamation with the SDF. At the ILP conference in 1896, a motion was passed to open new negotiations to this end. Hardie, strongly backed by Ramsay MacDonald, opposed the moves. Not because he was not a socialist, as some implied. His reasons were threefold. First, it would lose the ILP more votes at elections if identified with the more extreme socialism of the SDF. Second, he knew that a partnership with them would be a further barrier to his attempts to make links with the TUC, whose backing would be essential to the growth of a Labour Party. Third, he had long opposed the use of violence as a means to political ends as advocated by some of the SDF's members. It must be added that the two leaders, Hardie and Hyndman, strongly disliked each other. The negotiations eventually petered out, much to Hardie's relief. In 1897 Tom Mann resigned and departed for Australia.

CO-OPERATION WITH THE LIBERALS?

Meanwhile, a Liberal revival was taking place, as reflected in a series of victories in by-elections. Hardie knew that the ILP had to win votes from what he called "moderate Liberals". He made noises about co-operation with them over policies in which they had agreement, such as the eight-hour day, home rule, and the cultivation of vacant land. Hardie's ideological position could be confusing. At times he preached uncompromising socialism and condemned the Liberals as a bigger enemy than the Tories. At other times he bitterly opposed the SDF and expressed approval of certain Liberal proposals. Eleanor Marx, understandably, accused him of being "ideologically unstable". Hardie did believe in socialism as the long-term solution. But his short-term aims to win votes and to obtain the best possible reforms for the working class sometimes pushed him into saying favourable things about Liberal proposals.

His followers were also confused and he wrote two articles in the *Labour Leader* to make his position clear. In 1896 he published "Whither the Future of Labour – Socialism the Goal". He declared: "The Independent Labour Party can be no party to any arrangement with official Liberalism." He explained that the Liberals were built on capitalism, but the ILP on socialism, and hence the latter had to remain independent of the former. In 1898 he followed with "A Liberal–Labour Alliance?", reacting to some Liberal proposals for "an entente between Labour and advanced Liberals". Hardie pointed out that, as these advanced Liberals took the Liberal whip, they voted for policies which smashed strikes and facilitated employer lock-outs. Hardie made clear that giving approval to certain Liberal proposals in no way meant official alliance and in no way would the ILP compromise on its independence. He concluded, "To move parliament we must have agitation" against the government, but an alliance would prevent this.

INDUSTRIAL DISPUTES

Long articles do not promote agitation. Yet just at this time, when the ILP seemed distant from trade unions, the industrial scene changed and ILP agitation brought them closer. During the mid-1890s, a series of bitter labour disputes broke out. In the USA, a number of employers had formed into federations in order to take the initiative against trade unions by acting together and by recourse to the law. In Britain, engineering employers drew together in the Engineering and Employers'

Federation and in 1897 instigated a lock-out of members of the Amalgamated Society of Engineers. The ILP supported the engineers and Hardie backed them in print. In the same year, workers at the Penrhyan quarry in North Wales went on strike against a bullying owner. The TUC sent financial help while Hardie wrote, "The main question is the right of Lord Penrhyan to do as he pleases with his own, the rights of one man against the rights and liberties of 4000."

In the Christmas edition of the *Labour Leader,* he wrote angrily that he could not celebrate the festival while so many children were suffering the effects of the employers' actions and while professing Christians took no steps to stop them.

> I have known as a child what hunger means... A holocaust of every church building in Christendom tonight would be as an act of sweet savour in the sight of Him whose name is supposed to be worshipped within their walls. If the spiritually proud and pride-blinded professors of Christianity could only be made to feel and see that the Christ is here, ever present with us, and that they are urging on the stripes and binding the brow afresh with thorns and making shed tears of blood in a million homes. Surely the world could be made more sweet for the establishment of His kingdom. We have no right to a merry Christmas which so many of our fellows cannot share.

The engineers and quarry workers were defeated. Then came the miners in South Wales in March 1898 with a strike for a 20 per cent increase and the right to a minimum wage. Their determined action was an indication of their desperation, yet their Lib–Lab MPs were wary of supporting them against their Liberal paymasters. Hardie had no hesitation in setting up a strike fund and coming to the area – although in April 1898 he kept an appointment to speak at a women's conference at Ruskin Hall, Oxford, where he was accompanied by Lillie, who enjoyed herself.

The spring of 1898 proved a period of deaths which weighed heavily on Hardie. William Gladstone died in May. Hardie had spoken with Gladstone in the Commons but by this time they were political foes. Yet he retained an admiration for the old Liberal leader and praised him for refusing a peerage and his lack of pomposity. Then Lillie's mother, Sarah Wilson, fell terminally ill and Lillie nursed her at Lochnorris where, not long before she died, she made a contribution to the South Wales strike fund. Still in May, Hardie's friend Richard Pankhurst died suddenly in Manchester. Hardie felt he could not leave Lillie to attend the funeral. Perhaps, most tragically, Eleanor Marx committed suicide. She had become critical of Hardie's lack of commitment to Marxism but he always appreciated her encouragement. This surfeit of death upset Hardie but, at least, the passing of Lillie's mother gave her more time to accompany him to meetings.

Nonetheless, his thoughts were never far from the hundred thousand men on strike in South Wales. In the *Labour Leader,* Hardie pointed out that numbers had to resort to poor law relief, which entailed mindless stone-breaking. He added that the Liberals had upheld the law which removed the right to vote from those on relief. He could not resist a swipe at Christian mine-owners receiving £3,000 a year yet refusing to raise miners' wages to 22s. a week.

Eventually the miners were forced back to work. The strike was important to the ILP, which opened a number of new branches in the area. Hardie's presence and passion also made an impression and he got on particularly well with Welsh nonconformists. Sometimes he spoke at Sunday open-air meetings, which included hymns, prayers, and a sermon from Hardie. He had established himself in South Wales. But he was not just in Wales. His agitation took him all over the country visiting scores of places. He wrote to his friend Dave Lowe at the end of 1898: "Each place visited means meeting new people… and talking into the wee sma' 'oors with friends and faithful comrades each night. The 'reward' does not take the form of £.s.d. but of a fellowship rich and rare, which is of itself an inspiration."

On a larger scale, trade unions were realizing the need for more united and decisive political action against employers. Some acknowledged that Hardie's campaign against the weaknesses of Lib–Lab MPs was correct. These proposals were backed by the new secretary of the TUC, George Barnes, a member of the ILP.

LORD OVERTOUN

In January 1899 Hardie started taking breaks from his agitation with strikers and his vitally important negotiations with the TUC, in order to conduct a campaign in a Christian cause. That he should do so demonstrated how important his faith was to him, although some of his biographers give it little attention: Benn and Iain McLean a page and Morgan just a paragraph.

The target of his campaign was Lord Overtoun. According to his avid admirer Donald Carswell, Lord Overtoun was a man almost without fault. Born in 1843 as John Campbell White, he inherited his father's wealth and business. He was, Carswell eulogizes, "a man remarkable among his compeers. He filled the varied roles of merchant prince, county magnate, Churchman, evangelist and philanthropist."[3] A regular church-goer, a champion of keeping the Sabbath day free from work, he gave generously to numerous Christian charities. His contribution to industry, the church, and the Liberal Party was recognized when he was made Baron Overtoun in 1893. The huge mansion in which he lived still stands and, up to a few years ago, it was graced by his bust and portrait.

It was against this apparent paragon of virtue that Hardie launched a ferocious attack. He had been made aware of the other side of Overtoun when men from his chrome-making factory, the Shawfield Chemical Works, in Rutherglen, Glasgow, approached him and showed how the chemicals used there brought them out in rashes and adversely affected their lungs. Hardie undertook detailed investigations and then wrote a series of articles in the *Labour Leader* that he then brought together as a pamphlet entitled *White Slaves,* which sold tremendously in Glasgow and the west of Scotland.

He started with fulsome praise for Lord Overtoun, which was, of course, sarcasm: "Scarce a day passes in which his lordship is not found presiding or taking part in some gathering connected with a work of mercy or heading some deputation in the interests of morality… Whether it be a loan exhibition of heathen idols in the interests of foreign missions or a deputation to the Town Council to protest against the desecration of the sanctity of the Scottish Sabbath by the running of Sunday [tram] cars."

Hardie then listed just some of the numerous charities he supported and continued: "Not only the poor and needy at home but the dusky children of far-off lands who in spiritual darkness bow down to wood and stone are the objects of his beneficent solicitude. The sun in his daily journey round the globe shines continuously on some effort at removing sin and suffering which is inspired by Lord Overtoun. Little children of foreign lands are taught his name and lisp it in their prayers…"

Next Hardie cited a biblical text, "Therefore all things whatsoever ye would that men should do to you, do ye even so to them; for this is the law and the prophets" (Matthew 7:12).

Then came Hardie's description of the Overtoun chemical works (the italics are his):

I wish I could adequately describe a day's work, so that my readers could fully understand its horrors. The men on the day-shift go in to begin work at six in the morning. The vapours and fumes from the chemicals are about them all the time, eating away the cartilage of the nose and poisoning the blood so that the stomach in time will only contain certain kinds of food, and an intense desire for stimulants is generated. A dry dust floats in the atmosphere, which gets into the throat and produces an arid, burning feeling. The surroundings, as stated, are all of the gloomy, depressing kind. Once every hour, the two men who have to work a furnace have to draw their charge of molten chemicals. At this time, a sweet, poisonous gas is thrown off, which the men inhale every time they breathe. The charge is put into a small truck, which the men draw with a hook and empty at the appointed place. In some cases this is not more than a few feet from the furnace and the men have to work with the hot, glowing mass at their back and the roaring furnace in front. They have also to wheel the coal and chemicals with which the furnaces are charged. In addition, *once every fifteen minutes* the contents of the furnace have to be stirred up. This with wheeling the raw materials, charging the furnace, stirring the molten contents every fifteen minutes, drawing the charge every hour, the two men are kept constantly at work.

It hardly seems possible that any employer, let alone a Christian one, should impose such working conditions. But Hardie had not finished.

And this goes on all the day *without a break* until six o'clock in the evening – twelve weary, wretched hours. For it will scarcely be believed, but it is none the less true, that there are *no meal hours* allowed these men. From six in the morning until six at night without a stoppage. It sounds incredible, and yet it cannot be denied. Food has to be snatched in mouthfuls as best the men can whilst carrying on their never-ceasing task. With their hands soiled with the poisonous chemical they handle, inhaling a poison-laded atmosphere, they "dine" in the fashion here stated. Twelve hours every day, and *seven days every week*. For there is no rest for these men. If a man dares to stay away from work on Sunday to attend church or Chapel he is punished by being compelled to lose Monday's wages also. Lord Overtoun is a great man with the Sunday Rest and Lord's Day Observance Societies. When the Glasgow Corporation proposed to run Sunday cars to enable the citizens to get out from the streets and slums and to spend a few hours in the country a deputation from the societies named above waited upon the Town Council to enter an indignant protest against this description of the Lord's Day. Lord Overtoun headed that deputation!

Hardie then quoted Matthew's Gospel, which condemned hypocrites and ended, "ye outwardly appear righteous unto men, but within ye are full of hypocrisy and iniquity... Ye serpents, ye generation of vipers, how can ye escape the damnation of hell?" He emphasized that he was not against religion. Far from it, he stated, "I believe in Christ's gospel of love and brotherhood and service." But he feared that Overtoun's harshness and hypocrisy would drive people away from Christianity.

Given the terrible work conditions, Hardie said it could be expected that they were paid high wages in compensation. Not at all: "The wages are below those of a mason's labourer. The men who do labourers' work are paid *threepence* an hour; the furnacemen whose work I have been trying to describe are paid *fourpence* per hour." And they received no pay if sick and no pension. Hardie then cleverly changed tack again, declaring: "But Lord Overtoun can be generous when he pleases." He paid the Reverend John M'Neill, an evangelist to the poor, £1,000 a year. Hardie then challenged Overtoun's beneficiaries to insist that their lord bring in an eight-hour day, a six-day week, a minimum wage of 6*d*. an hour, and proper sanitary conditions.

Hardie's pamphlet was a sensation. As Carswell said, Overtoun was greatly disturbed "due to the extreme publicity achieved by the agitators throughout all Scotland".[4] To the surprise of many clergy, Lord Overtoun made no reply. How could he? As even Carswell admitted, "These disclosures create a most painful impression, the more so in that they were apparently true and could elicit no substantial and categorical denial from Lord Overtoun."[5] All that Carswell could say in his defence was that the Sunday labour was justified because of "the inexorable demands of economic law"[6] – so capitalism's laws were superior to Christian ones! Further, "Lord Overtoun maintained a dignified reticence in the face of the malicious campaign."[7]

But if Overtoun kept silent, those who benefited from his largess did not. Many clergy and Christian workers hurled abuse at Hardie from pulpits and in prints, accusing him of being an atheist, of trying to undermine a forthcoming evangelistic campaign in Glasgow led by Dwight Moody and John M'Neill and of trying to stir up an unjustified scandal against Overtoun. The printers of the *Labour Leader* were so afraid of threats not to employ them that they refused to print any more of Hardie's writings. Hardie had written scathingly: "Clergymen living separated from their wives should be very chary in their reference to scandals." This was taken by a Reverend Paterson – one of Hardie's critics – as a reference to himself and he promised legal action. Hardie was prepared and Paterson withdrew his threat. A minority of Christians, especially Christian socialists, did defend Hardie and asked for the truth about Overtoun.

The attacks were so numerous, continuous, and personal that Hardie replied in another pamphlet headed *More About Overtoun*. He wrote:

The first pamphlet has been variously characterised as a "Vile

Attack", "A Socialist Attack" and "Atheist Attack" not only on Lord
Overtoun but on Christianity, and in particular on the coming
campaign for the salvation of Glasgow. My 20 years' record as an
active, albeit voluntary and unpaid worker in temperance and
religious work is answer sufficient to these statements for those who
know me. I have great faith in the power of Christ's gospel – which
our churches so shamefully pervert – as a regenerating force over
the hearts and lives of men, and because of this I want it to have
a fair chance of doing its work, and that it cannot have so long as
it is burdened by such weights as Lord Overtoun.... D. L. Moody
and John M'Neill may come and use all their platform arts and
gifts, but Glasgow will not be moved to listen, unless it be to ribald
mirth. Whilst they talk, the thoughts of the listeners will be on
Lord Overtoun and his slaughter-house at Shawfield. John M'Neill's
thousand a year earned by the sacrifice of men, will stand between
him and his hearers; nay will weigh down his own heart and spirit.
He had a first taste, at the Free Church Assembly on Wednesday,
of what the future holds in store for him. If even his own Christian
brethren howled him down, what mercy can he expect at the hands
of working men?

Pressure had been put on Hardie by some clergy to withdraw
or end his campaign. He responded angrily, saying "Servility,
hypocrisy, mammon worship, the cult of respectability and
the fear of truth have eaten like canker worms the marrow
from their bones." He knew that some were uneasy and wrote,
"If half-a-dozen of the clergy of Glasgow were prepared to
sacrifice all for Christ's sake, the worst would be past. I am
asked to remain silent concerning a great wrong because if it
be made public it may damage Christianity. As if God could
be hood-winked, as if Christ would bless an effort founded on
a lie, and financed by gold stained with the tears and blood of
those for whom He died."
The attacks on Hardie continued: but not from Overtoun.

Soon after, he made substantial increases to the workers' wages, improved conditions, and largely abolished Sunday working. As Hardie himself pointed out, Overtoun was one of the leading employers in the chemical industry and his example would be followed by others. Hardie had won a remarkable victory.

As Professor Morgan puts it, Hardie had "exposed the exploitation and evils of private capitalism at the expense of Lord Overtoun".[8] This exposure owed most to Hardie's skill as a writer. He did not produce academic or theoretical books. But his ability as a writer of articles and pamphlets has been overlooked. Of course, writing several pieces every week, often in railway compartments, often while cold and wet, did mean a variability in the quality of his enormous output. But, at his best, he had a direct style which graphically portrayed the poverty, inequalities, and injustices in Britain. The Overtoun pamphlets, in particular, are works of power which frightened the wealthy and powerful.

The Overtoun affair also illustrated, again, the centrality of Christianity to Hardie. He spoke of "the power of Christ's gospel as a regenerating force over the hearts and lives of men". He emphasized the death of Christ as the means of forgiveness. His religion was not that of an impersonal God but of one who wanted to enter the lives of individuals. In contrast to the likes of Overtoun, he also saw Christianity as about abolishing poverty and evil working conditions. Indeed, he claimed that he was repeating the teaching of Jesus when he condemned those who ignored the social gospel as hypocrites. Further, their hypocrisy was a barrier to belief by working-class people because they perceived that their so-called "betters" did not apply Jesus' teaching – such as the Sermon on the Mount – to themselves.

Benn adds the point that Hardie was "conscious of what unmitigated greed did to the environment".[9] In the Overtoun factory, he perceived the harm the chemicals did both to individual health and also to the surrounding air. He pointed out that the factory tipped poisonous liquids into the river. Earlier he had accused other companies of spoiling the purity of nearby rivers. In similar fashion, he condemned Sir Thomas Lipton for using putrid fruits in his food products. Hardie was not the only one concerned about the fouling of the environment but he was one of the first. He also had a modern ring when he attacked unscrupulous business people such as Lipton for spending their ill-gotten gains on luxury yachts.

Labour Representation Committee

While the Overtoun affair was hitting the Scottish headlines, Hardie was also forging links between the TUC and the ILP. This was not easy for, despite the position of George Barnes and despite the changing industrial climate, the larger trade unions were still loyal to their own Lib–Lab MPs and the Liberal Party. Hardie therefore made little mention of socialism and put his case on the need for the trade unions and the ILP to share independent parliamentary representation.

He found a path to the centre of trade unionism through the Scottish Trade Union Congress (STUC), formed as late as 1897. In its chair was his old friend Bob Smillie, who must have played a part in inviting Hardie to its 1899 conference. The STUC contained a number of union delegates who were also members of the ILP and were both sympathetic to him and worried about the threats from employers. The delegates would also have been aware of Hardie's courage in standing up for the workers so badly treated by Lord Overtoun in Glasgow. Negotiations started, and in January 1900 the two sides agreed to pursue united action in regard to parliamentary representation. This was restricted to Scotland but, as Morgan explained, "For the first time, he [Hardie] had gained a clear decision from organised trade unionists to pursue parliamentary representation on an independent basis."[10]

Meanwhile, south of the border at the TUC conference in Plymouth in September 1899, the Amalgamated Society of Railway Servants, a large union which increasingly felt the need for protection against employers, put forward a motion proposing joint action with socialist bodies to further political representation. The large unions, particularly those of coal and cotton, opposed it and the implied attack on their Lib–Lab MPs. Smaller unions, often of unskilled workers, supported it, as did some larger ones. Margaret Bondfield stated that her small Shop Assistants' Union could not promote satisfactory legislation on its own and backed the motion. Over twenty years later, she was to be the first woman cabinet minister in a Labour government.

The motion was carried decisively. Thus both the STUC and the larger British TUC had moved in the same direction. It was agreed to meet at the Memorial Hall, London, in February 1900 with 129 delegates from the TUC, the STUC, the ILP, the Fabians, and the SDF. A trade unionist and Liberal MP, W. C. Steadman, was in the chair but the presence of major union members from the Railway Servants and the Gasworkers, plus a number of ILP members, was sufficient to allow Hardie to dominate. Hardie was sometimes accused of being difficult to work with. If so, on this occasion he overcame differences with certain delegates for the sake of the common good. Hardie calmly brought the differing sections together. A proposal to restrict Labour parliamentary candidates to working men or to socialists was defeated with his backing. Hardie personally wrote the vital amendment that there should be set up "a distinct Labour group in Parliament, who shall have their own whips and agree upon their policy, which must embrace a readiness to co-operate with any party which for the time being may be engaged in promoting legislation in the direct interests of Labour".

It meant that the new group would be independent of other parties but prepared to co-operate with them. It was broad enough to include both labourites and socialists without the latter being dominant. Hardie displayed enormous tact and the amendment was carried unanimously. The papers were full of the war in South Africa, and the negotiations in the Memorial Hall received little coverage. The Fabian historian Margaret Cole wrote that the motion "is not very exciting, it does not contain a clarion call to action, or even express a policy".[11] But Hardie had found a way of uniting different parts of the working class and in so doing was shaping political history. James Maxton, later a Labour MP, explained that Hardie's immediate concern was to create "a great workers' political party formed by a confederation of the trade unions and the cooperative societies".[12] Not just Hardie of course: without the support of certain trade union delegates, he could not have been successful. From the ILP, Bruce Glasier was important in that he now rejected the more extremist tactics of the SDF and allied himself with Hardie's ethical and gradual path to socialism. Ramsay MacDonald was also a capable negotiator.

A Labour Representation Committee (the LRC) was established to oversee the new approach. Its twelve members were to consist of seven trade unionists and five from the so-called socialist bodies (two from the ILP and the SDF and one from the Fabians). The trade union representation was small in proportion to their huge numbers. Hardie is given the credit (or blame) for this, although it is not clear how it happened. The SDF later dropped out. Hardie was one of the ILP's representatives and soon took a leading role. Then Ramsay MacDonald was appointed secretary – with an office in his own house – a post he retained until 1911. The trade unions – notwithstanding that some of the larger unions were not sympathetic to this new development – provided the numbers and much of the money, but it was the ILP that initially took the leadership.

Yet within a few months, in April 1900, Hardie resigned as chair of the ILP, to be succeeded by Bruce Glasier, whose friendship with Hardie survived a number of differences over tactics. He made a sincere speech of thanks to Hardie in which he drew attention to Hardie's faithfulness to the working class to which he belonged.

Why did he resign? Hardie could be a skilled negotiator and chair but it was a burden. He much preferred to be an agitator, travelling the country, staying with friends, preaching socialism, and keeping close to the grass roots.

But there was another reason, the outcome of which, ironically, would tie him to a role and restrict his movements. It appears he also wanted to return to Parliament, where he realized he still had a role to play in putting the condition of the people on the political agenda. In 1898 he said at a public meeting in Glasgow: "To move parliament we must have agitation. There is no other way of creating that public opinion of which we are told that parliament is the vehicle of expression. I admit freely that agitation conducted from the floor of the House of Commons is the most effective, and from this it follows we ought to aim at getting men in." A general election came more quickly than he anticipated and before the new LRC was ready. The Tory (now more often called the Conservative) government, aiming to cash in on its success in the Boer War, called an election for October 1900.

CHAPTER 6

SOUTH AFRICA AND SOUTH WALES; AN MP AGAIN, 1900–1905

In October 1899, war erupted in South Africa, with the Republic of Transvaal under President Paul Kruger defying Britain. Its antecedents went back a number of years. Perhaps the starting point was the discovery in 1886 of a huge gold mine in Transvaal, which attracted thousands of *uitlanders* (foreigners), many of whom were British. But they were not allowed to vote and were heavily taxed and, as they grew in number, became a potential source of rebellion. Following the Jameson Raid, instigated by the English-born South African politician Cecil Rhodes, which failed to take the Transvaal capital of Pretoria, tensions mounted between the Boers of Dutch origin and the British, who ruled much of South Africa.

The war, in which the Orange Free State sided with Transvaal, provoked a tremendous outbreak of jingoism in Britain with Queen Victoria giving her open support to it. The Conservatives were in power, with the colonial secretary, Joseph Chamberlain, in charge of the war. After initial victories by the Boers, he sent out thousands of troops and both sides suffered heavy losses.

The Liberals were divided, with some, including David Lloyd George and John Morley, opposing the war. The Independent Labour Party (ILP) was strongly against it. The Fabian Society refused to support or oppose it and Ramsay MacDonald, one of its best-known members and fiercely against the war, resigned. Robert Blatchford, the famed socialist author, and once a professional soldier, rejoiced in every battle. The public largely turned against the ILP and when its Glasgow branch agreed to steward an anti-war meeting at which Lloyd George was speaking – with Hardie as chief steward – violence erupted and the offices of the *Labour Leader* were ransacked. Hardie was not one to avoid trouble and preached against the war from the back of wagons. Sometimes he was attacked by pro-war rowdies, with the police doing little to protect him. Even Quakers reading aloud the teachings of Jesus were shouted down. But there were occasional successes. He debated at the Oxford Union, where he refused to wear evening dress, and by five votes won a motion condemning the war.

In 1898 Hardie had already made his position clear: "I do not say we should never fight. As Rider Haggard has said, 'The Almighty has endowed us with life and doubtless meant us to defend it.' War in the past was inevitable when the sword constituted the only court of appeal. But the old reasons for war have passed away... Today they fight to extend markets and no empire can stand being based solely on the sordid considerations of trade and commerce."

To be sure, Hardie was led into some foolish statements. He seemed to regard President Kruger as a kindly local hero. Margaret Cole commented that "Hardie even went as far as to talk of Kruger as if that narrow-minded nigger-driver were something only less than Jesus Christ".[1] Because Transvaal was a republic, he seemed to think it was democratic and appeared ignorant that Kruger, when re-elected president in 1898, had dismissed the head of the judicature and become a virtual dictator.

But Hardie attacked the war brilliantly in the *Labour Leader*. His friend William Stewart recorded that "Hardie was wielding his pen with a skill and prowess such as he had never exhibited before".[2] He led on three fronts. First, he highlighted the number of deaths. Early in the war, he wrote after one campaign, "Over 1,000 men dead and buried in the Veldt; 5,000 wounded and in hospital: 3,000 prisoners in Pretoria and the real fighting not yet begun."

Second, he saw the war as basically created by capitalism, in which native South Africans, white and black, were already being exploited by British investors, mine-owners, and speculators. Now they backed war in order to exploit Transvaal. He explained in the *Labour Leader*, "The war is a capitalist war. The British merchant hopes to secure markets for his goods, the investor an outlay for his capital, the speculator more fools out of whom to make money, and the mining companies cheaper labour and increased dividends." The profits of British companies rose but Hardie was quick to point out that the working class not only provided many of the foot soldiers who were slain abroad but also suffered economically at home. With the government desperate for coal, mine-owners raised their prices. The increases also applied to domestic coal, bringing great hardship to the poor. Hardie was not the only one to criticize the war-makers but he was the most persistent. Moreover, at the *Labour Leader*, he recruited journalists who were able to show how members of companies making money from the war were in public positions where they could influence colonial policy.

Third, once again he savaged clergy who supported the war. "He, by his office stands forth as the representative of Him who taught the doctrine of non-resistance, even when attacked, as an integral part of His philosophy of life... When clergymen advocate or support a war like the one now being waged they but proclaim themselves infidels who do not believe the gospel... Nowhere is Mammon more firmly seated than in the church."

Hardie feared and hated war. He later wrote that the two main aims of socialism were "the abolition of war" and "public ownership".[3] He had no doubt that war was anti-Christian. The horror of the needless massacres in South Africa remained with him. He now foresaw more wars and his regular involvement in Socialist Internationals was partly to persuade working-class people not to participate in killing each other.

For the sake of continuity, it can be said that the war ended in May 1902. Britain theoretically won but was generous in the settlement with Transvaal. The war had cost Britain about £222 million which, as opponents made clear, could have been put to better use in Britain. By this time, the public mood had changed. The revelation – after denials – that British troops had run concentration camps for civilians, in which over 20,000 women and children died, mainly from disease, horrified previous supporters of the war. At least some conceded that the ILP had been right.

GENERAL ELECTION OF 1900

Let us return to 1900. While striving to cash in on some military successes in South Africa, the Conservative government suddenly called a general election for October 1900 – the "khaki election". The odds were against the ILP. It had only just come to the agreement with the Trade Union Congress (TUC) to set up the Labour Representation Committee (LRC). It was short of money and had to fight the election while the war still raged.

Hardie looked for a constituency. Both Preston and Merthyr Tydfil made approaches (candidates could still stand in more than one constituency) and Hardie accepted both. The fact that Hardie had received £150 from George Cadbury, the Quaker chocolate manufacturer, toward election expenses enabled him to stand in two places. Both were places which elected two MPs and so a party could put up two candidates.

Preston was a Conservative stronghold and not known as ILP territory and Hardie's interest remains a mystery. He may have been persuaded by John Penney, a Preston man, and now secretary of the ILP.

Merthyr Tydfil knew Hardie because of his involvement in their recent miners' strike. In Merthyr itself and in Aberdare there were strong trade councils with prominent socialist members, including iron and steel workers, railway workers, and other occupations as well as miners. In September 1900 they were responsible for nominating Hardie as their LRC candidate. Hardie had socialist and nonconformist support but the miners were not necessarily on his side. Their Lib–Lab MPs, particularly William Brace, the vice-president of the South Wales Miners' Federation, were popular. Further, their union had not yet joined the TUC.

Preston polled a day before Merthyr. Hardie made no secret of his opposition to the war nor of his support of public ownership, and made much of his temperance programme. His strategy was to draw votes from the Liberals. The two Conservatives won easily, although Hardie managed a respectable 4,834.

He had been campaigning in both constituencies and, with Preston completed, immediately made for Wales. For the first time, he got into a car and toured the polling stations, although it did have to be pushed up steep Welsh hills. He was heartened by groups of miners who waited in the rain to cheer him. His opponents attacked his anti-imperialism but the constituency also contained some who held on to a pacifist tradition, particularly the much respected Reverend Henry Richard. But the strongest factors in Hardie's favour were to do with the weaknesses of the opposition. The two Liberal candidates and sitting members did not get on. Pritchard Morgan was an extreme imperialist and capitalist. D. A. Thomas was against the war. Although a pit-owner, he was sympathetic to the miners' well-being and seemed to regard Hardie as a more co-operative partner than Pritchard Morgan. The Conservatives were in such disarray that they selected a candidate who had never been to Merthyr and made his way to Newcastle-upon-Tyne by mistake. By the time he reached Wales, he was too late to register.

Thomas headed the poll comfortably with 8,508. Hardie came second with 5,745, with many voting for both him and Thomas as a pair. Pritchard Morgan made only 4,004. Hardie was back in the Commons. It was a sensational and unexpected victory. Hardie was lifted onto the shoulders of his supporters. He had been accompanied by Lillie in the campaigning and he recorded, "That night from the hotel window, in response to cries loud and long-continued, I witnessed a sight I had never hoped to see this side of the pearly gate. My wife was making a speech to the delighted crowd." Bruce Glasier read the news in a newspaper on the train back from campaigning in Lancashire. He kissed his wife and baby and they danced in the train.

Back in Cumnock, they were met at the station by local miners, who had known and supported Hardie for years. They took the harnesses from the horses and dragged the couple through the streets in a wagon. Later they entertained them as guests of honour at the town hall. Hardie was never elected to any constituency in Scotland but, until his death, he retained the respect and loyalty of many whose lives he had striven to improve. Stewart recorded that one rose to pay tribute, saying that "had their townsman [Hardie] cared to turn his talents to personal advantage, he might today have been a wealthy man… But he was not built that way. He had all his life been creating agencies through which the spirit of democracy might find expression."[4] Hardie valued most the opinions of those nearest to him. Interestingly, just at this time he could have indeed been a wealthy man when a woman from Belfast offered to leave him £20,000 if he would campaign against popery. He declined.

He was glad to be home for a few weeks. James had just finished his apprenticeship as an engineer. Duncan was starting in the same trade. Nan had left school and was helping her mother with the household duties. In addition, she listened to her father's experiences and welcomed him beginning to use her as one of his secretaries. She collected stamps for a charity and one day complained that he had received only forty-two letters that day. She was the one who would follow him as an elected socialist.

BACK IN THE COMMONS

Back in London, Hardie could no longer lodge with Frank Smith. For 6s. 6d. a week, he found a place at Neville's Court, off Fleet Street and so close to the office of the *Labour Leader,* walkable to Westminster and accessible to London railway stations, particularly Kings Cross. Neville's Court was a medieval structure and Hardie had what was basically a large room with partitions for a bedroom and bathroom. It was snug and comfortable and he liked it. It was here he entertained socialists from all over Britain and the world. They may have been surprised that Hardie did all his own cleaning, cooking, and shoeblacking. Not many MPs did that.

Morgan asserts that Neville's Court became the "nearest he came to having a home for the remainder of his tortured life".[5] Far from it. He only spent parliamentary sessions in London

– if that. Home was Cumnock – when in London he longed to be with his family and when in Cumnock he sometimes wrote about the relaxation and peace he found there.

The ILP had started to pay Hardie £150 a year as an MP. This was insufficient to maintain homes in both Scotland and England and to undertake constituency duties in Wales. The Miners' Federation paid its MPs £350 a year. Finance was a constant personal and family problem.

Fortunately, he obtained some secretarial help from the daughter of a Welsh friend. Margaret Symons, married to a New Zealand landowner, lived in Hampstead and offered her services on a half-time basis. An educated woman, she sorted out his parliamentary papers. She was also a "new woman" and must have felt some conflict in receiving little financial reward.

In the Commons, the Conservatives had won by a substantial majority, with the Liberals still split over the war which still raged. The eighty Irish nationalist MPs, whose main interest was home rule, also tended to oppose the war. The ILP had fought only eight seats. Another six stood under the LRC, which, attracting trade unionists' votes, polled well but only Richard Bell (who took over the chair of the LRC in 1902) of the Amalgamated Society of Railway Servants was elected. Bell was soon claimed by the Liberals, although he continued to admire Hardie. Hardie was alone again and, despite all the declarations of the LRC, there was no Labour Party to be whipped as an independent group.

Initially, Hardie seemed to flounder. Surprisingly, he put out feelers to John Morley, the talented pro-Boer Liberal MP, to John Burns, who put himself under the Liberal wing but still had a working-class following, and to the lawyer Lloyd George, asking them to lead the Labour group. Some of his biographers have seen this as Hardie going back on his insistence on being independent of the Liberal Party and even as surrendering to them. Not so. His letters make it clear that he wanted these individuals to leave the Liberal Party and to bring radical Liberals into the Labour fold. He wrote in an open letter to Lloyd George that Liberalism "is now a council of despair. You know its real leaders better than I do – its Mammon worshipping Roseberys, Haldanes, Fowlers, Asquiths, and their like, and the abject, spiritless creatures who make up the bulk of their following in parliament." Morley, Burns, and Lloyd George all refused.

Hardie, on his own, went back to his old tactics of raising important issues, which the Commons usually ignored, and hoping for press publicity.

A foreign newspaper had asked several public figures in Britain what was the chief danger in the new century. Hardie replied, "Militarism! It distracts attention from social questions, subordinates the rights of the civilian to the imperious rule of the soldier, increases taxes, interferes with trade and commerce and glorifies war… It is a contradiction of the principles of Christianity." At the first opportunity he rose to condemn the Boer War and, after Queen Victoria died in January 1901, he complained about the military display at her funeral, adding, "The dead body of England's Queen was made a recruiting sergeant to help the military business." Hardie was soon ruled out of order when he claimed that her death gave the opportunity "to recommend the office of hereditary rule be abolished".

Caroline Benn says that "Hardie's democratic commitment increased with time: 'I owe no allegiance to any hereditary rule'. As he grew older, he grew bolder, and regularly refused to stand for the national anthem."[6]

Once again, he criticized the continuance of poverty and inequality. He opposed a large pension for a Boer War commander and asked what was available for private soldiers coming back wounded. "The workhouse," shouted some

Conservatives. He wrote a powerful pamphlet entitled *Can a Man be a Christian on a Pound a Week?* After concluding he could not, he pointed to Seebohm Rowntree's study in York showing 30 per cent of the population were below the poverty line. He was an early supporter of free school meals.

Hardie always had a concern for vulnerable children. Interesting was his condemnation of baby farming. Children were often placed privately with foster parents (usually women) for dubious care known as baby farming. The private foster mothers sometimes took out insurance, murdered the children and claimed the money. In 1870, a woman was executed for such murders. The Infant Life Protection Act (1872) placed investigative duties on councils, but they were never implemented. A further act in 1897 was no more effective, hence Hardie's public concern for the safety of the children. In the late 1960s, research on private fostering concluded it was still "a private market with virtually no controls on it".[7] It was not until 2004 that the government gave local authorities real powers, although the extent to which they have applied them has yet to be shown.

Hardie won a place in a ballot for private members' bills and on 23 April 1901 put forward the first ever motion for a socialist commonwealth. It blamed poverty on private ownership and called for a "Socialist Commonwealth founded upon the common ownership of land and capital, production for use and not for profit, and equality of opportunity for every citizen". He only had twenty minutes but was not shouted down and indeed, members and press listened carefully. He declared: "The House and the British nation know to their cost the danger which comes from allowing men to grow rich and permitting them to use their wealth to corrupt the press, to silence the pulpit, to degrade our national life, and to bring shame and reproach upon a great people in order that a few unscrupulous scoundrels might be able to add to their ill-gotten gains." Of course, Hardie won few supporters and his bill confirmed him as a socialist. Outside Parliament, Hardie argued that municipal socialism was underway with property valued at £500 million passing into public hands as ILP and LRC councillors exerted an influence.

The trouble for Hardie was that he was keeping three political balls in the air. One, he believed in socialism. Two, he wanted Liberals to vote for LRC candidates but they were often put off by his socialism. Indeed, in some by-elections LRC candidates asked him to stay away. Three, he put out feelers to Liberals such as Lloyd George but this aroused the wrath of some socialists. But he never wavered on his insistence that the independence of the LRC had to be maintained. Not surprisingly, he sometimes confused his followers.

BY-ELECTION VICTORIES

As mentioned, not all trade unions had backed the LRC. But, outside Parliament, trade union attitudes were to be profoundly affected by events on a small railway line in Hardie's constituency. The Taff Vale Railway carried coal to Cardiff. After a strike, the owners sued the unions for loss of profits: the law lords eventually found in their favour in 1901. The Taff Vale Railway Company won £23,000 plus costs. The judgment meant any trade union could be sued for action which damaged employers' interests.

Trade unions realized that only new legislation could reverse the decision, and support for the LRC began to increase. In early 1901 only forty-one unions representing 350,000 members backed the LRC. By 1903 membership was 850,000, that is over half the membership of the TUC.

The LRC renewal was reflected in by-elections. In 1902 a vacancy occurred at Clitheroe in Lancashire, a strong Liberal stronghold. The local weavers' union put forward David

Shackleton, a union official and local councillor, to stand under the LRC banner. The Liberal candidate, a pro-Boer radical, refused to stand against him. The Conservatives failed to obtain a candidate, so Shackleton was elected unopposed.

The following year, there was no danger of a lack of opponents at Woolwich, which had been held by the Conservatives, who attracted working-class votes. The LRC candidate was Will Crooks, an elected member of the London County Council. Crooks had spent part of his childhood in the workhouse and, as an adult, was elected as a guardian of the very same institution, as recounted in his biography *From Workhouse to Westminster*. Another guardian was George Lansbury – they were both Christians and temperance men – and together they carried out a famous policy of reform for that workhouse. In the by-election, Crooks won with a stunning majority of over 3,000. This was also the year in which Philip Snowden took over as president of the ILP – yet another who was both a strong temperance man and an active Christian.

Later that year, another vacancy occurred at Barnard Castle in County Durham, which had long been held for the Liberals by members of the Pease family. In 1900, Arthur Henderson, born in Glasgow but brought up in Newcastle-upon-Tyne, had been the election agent for Joseph Pease. Secretary of the iron-founders' union and a former councillor in Newcastle, he decided to stand himself for the LRC. Pease died and in a closely and bitterly fought contest between Conservatives, Liberals, and LRC Henderson won by forty-seven votes, with the Liberals finishing bottom.

For some reason, modern biographers of Hardie have argued that Crooks and Henderson were more Liberal than socialist. Iain McLean wrote, "Crooks was no socialist."[8] Kenneth Morgan asserted of him that "he associated exclusively with Liberals when he arrived at Westminster".[9] Yet he supported the LRC and its policy of independence from the Liberals, and both outside and inside the Commons was closely associated with George Lansbury (elected in 1910) and there could be no more out and out socialist than Lansbury.

Of Henderson, McLean wrote that there "was no love lost between him and the ILP".[10] Yet Henderson attended ILP and LRC meetings. In his biography, it is recorded that, at a TUC congress, "There was a socialist resolution moved, demanding the nationalisation of the means of production, distribution and exchange", which he supported, and that "He admired Hardie immensely".[11] Once elected, he became a loyal and important member of the Labour group and years later Henderson became leader of the Labour Party. He was no Liberal.

Hardie was no longer alone. Despite the desertion of Bell, the Labour group had four members. Hardie, Crooks, Henderson, and Shackleton made up a competent group. They all spoke in the Commons, with Hardie in the fore. He attacked the Aliens Bill of 1905 by which the government was trying to keep out poor Jewish refugees fleeing from Russian Poland. The arguments have something in common with those made in 2008 by a government determined to reduce the number of asylum-seekers approaching Britain – but this time Labour was the government.

As before, Hardie, supported by the experience of his colleagues, raised the issue of unemployment. He acidly pointed out that, far from increasing employment, the Boer War was followed by a slump. Hardie, in conjunction with Will Crooks and George Lansbury, called for farm colonies for those out of work. Lansbury was the chief mover. An American soap millionaire, Joseph Fels, had sought him out and wanted to help. When Lansbury escorted him back to the railway station, he asked Fels what class he was travelling. The reply was: "Third, because there isn't any fourth."[12] Lansbury was convinced he was genuine and Fels eventually bought land for the Poplar board of guardians to develop as farm schemes.

In the long run they failed because the men were too far from their familiar environments and drifted back when local jobs became available. But Lansbury and Crooks pointed out that some men, equipped with new skills, found jobs on farms, for instance in Canada.

Meanwhile Hardie's repeated attacks, along with huge demonstrations in the large cities, did prompt the Conservative government to pass a feeble Unemployed Workmen's Act (1905). It permitted local district committees to organize public work for the unemployed but did not provide the money for their wages. In three months, the Poplar board of guardians received applications covering over 10,000 people. George Lansbury led a march of 6,000 women to the offices of the Local Government Board. A. J. Balfour received a deputation but offered nothing but sympathy. At least it gained large press coverage.

Outside Parliament, the four MPs were part of the LRC committee, whose secretary was the capable Ramsay MacDonald. Arthur Henderson's biographer, Mary Agnes Hamilton, described MacDonald and Henderson as "A racehorse and a cart horse, a tiger and an elephant", and continued: "they complemented each other admirably. The rapid development of the committee's work, and its growing appeal were mainly due to this unique combination. There could be no achievement unless the trade unions came in; there was no man better calculated to pull them in than Henderson."[13] MacDonald, although not yet an MP, by his efficiency, intelligence, and charm made links with a range of politicians.

Changes within the Liberal Party

But there was one matter in which MacDonald excluded even Henderson, namely a pact with the Liberals. Politics was changing. The Conservatives were backing a trade policy of protectionism in order to help British industries. The Liberals, and the small Labour group, gave their traditional support to free trade. More dramatically, the Liberals, under the leadership of Sir Henry Campbell-Bannerman, were embracing state welfare.

The Liberal change from a party which opposed state interference to one which backed it was partly a compliment to Hardie's agitation both inside and outside the Commons. He had put unemployment and poverty on the public agenda. But not just Hardie and his colleagues. Among a number of studies of poverty, three had had a huge impact: Charles Booth, *Life and Labour of the People* (1889), William Booth, *Darkest England and the Way Out* (1890), and Seebohm Rowntree, *Poverty. A Study of Town Life* (1901). These reports certainly influenced some MPs.

Also making themselves heard were a number of clergymen, some of whom already had grass-roots experience of knowing those in poverty. F. B. Meyer, as mentioned, was a leading nonconformist who became president of the Baptist Union. In Leicester and then London he had run large-scale projects to help the socially deprived. Numbers of working-class residents were drawn into his church in Lambeth and in 1905 he declared, "Men are ceasing to believe that the individual is the true unit of society, and that the law of social progress is to be found in rivalry and competition. They are becoming conscious of the possibility of a common life and destiny."[14] Meyer had much sympathy for socialism but remained Liberal and urged the party to deal with poverty through statutory action.

The Conservatives' Education Act (1902) put state schools in England and Wales fully under local authorities, with the addition that voluntary schools run by the Church of England and the Roman Catholic Church would also receive help from the rates. That the state help was given only to these two denominations which roused the ire of nonconformists, and the Liberal Party led the opposition. Hardie agreed – indeed, he thought state education should be secular, but the large and united Liberal Party was in the fore.

Thus the Liberal Party was becoming one of social reform and began shaping plans for old-age pensions, state housing, and help for the unemployed for the next election. All this may have been a compliment to the years of agitation by the ILP and the LRC. The fear was that the Liberal Party was taking their ground and perhaps their votes. The wily MacDonald thought that the best hope for the LRC was to co-operate, not compete, with the Liberals. In January 1903 he started secret negotiations with the Liberals' chief whip, Herbert Gladstone, with the Liberals agreeing not to oppose the LRC in thirty constituencies. The hope was to keep out the Conservatives in these places and let in the LRC. It was, as McLean observed, "a momentous event in the early history of the Labour Party".[15] But it was risky in that it could have aroused enormous opposition within both parties. MacDonald therefore told no one except Hardie. McLean praises Hardie for swallowing "a deal of which he almost certainly did disapprove... when it really mattered, Keir Hardie was perfectly well able to follow his head rather than his heart".[16] It was not as straightforward as that, although he always put the interests of the party before himself; Hardie was feeling ill throughout much of 1903. Almost certainly he did not accompany MacDonald to the meetings with Gladstone. His justification to himself was probably that it was not an official alliance with the Liberals and did not undermine the independence of the LRC. Interestingly, at this time he wrote an article on the class war and, as usual, rejected violence between classes. He noted the growing social conscience moving some middle-class politicians toward welfare reform and stated, "No revolution can succeed which has not public opinion behind it." The role of socialists such as himself, in and out of Parliament, was to change public opinion, even that of the Liberal Party.

HARDIE ILL

For years Hardie toiled long hours, travelled all over Britain in all weathers, maintained an enormous correspondence, and spoke every week at meetings – not to mention being an MP. It was almost commonplace for observers to comment on his tiredness and premature old age. In 1900, soon after returning to the Commons, he felt ill but continued working at the same pace. In July 1901, he again complained of pain but did not seek treatment. In 1902 matters got worse. Nan was taken ill – according to one author, with appendicitis complicated by peritonitis and pleurisy. These illnesses often led to death in Victorian times. Hardie went home for weeks and gladly did the housework and washing while Lillie provided the nursing care. Gradually Nan recovered.

Soon after returning to London, he was summoned to Glasgow, where both his mother and stepfather had been taken ill. He got there in time to speak with them but they died within an hour of each other. Mary had loved him as fully and as positively as any mother could. Her passing left a great void in his life. At home, his son Duncan sometimes suffered from erysipelas, an infectious disease of the skin. Toward the end of the year, Hardie's friends persuaded him to take a break – if it can be called that – to a meeting of European socialists in Belgium. In its parliament building, the police noticed his down-at-heel clothing and arrested him as a suspected anarchist.

During January 1903, he was working at full stretch again but colleagues considered something was wrong. In July he collapsed after an open-air meeting and rested at Cumnock. Here he may have been worried by his son Jamie, who was working away from home and was accumulating gambling

debts. Later Hardie paid the considerable debts, apparently
much to the annoyance of Lillie, who still struggled financially.
Jamie took a job as an engineer on a merchant ship. Hardie
returned to the London fray and collapsed again. Diagnosed
as having appendicitis, he was taken to a London clinic, where
an operation was completed successfully. He received a letter
of good wishes from Edward VII, who had suffered previously
from both Hardie's sharp tongue and the same illness. One can
imagine Hardie gruffly conceding that the letter was "really a
very human document".

Lillie had travelled to London immediately and her care
and concern moved him. A public appeal to pay his medical
expenses was over-subscribed, which demonstrated that he
was still held in affection by many citizens, especially working-
class ones. The money even allowed him and Lillie to convalesce
in Falmouth but he made sure that, for Hogmanay, they were
back in Scotland. In early 1904 Hardie continued to stay and
enjoy life in his beloved Cumnock.

Just at this juncture, however, he lost control of the *Labour
Leader*. It had lost something of its unique combination of
seriousness and socialistic evangelism, probably because its
main contributor had been unwell, and both the circulation
and advertising revenue had dropped. There was also an
understandable criticism from some ILP members that it was
too much Hardie's paper and too little that of the movement.
In January 1904 he handed over control to the ILP without
public complaint. But he was hurt that, having put his time,
his money, and his life into it ever since he started it in 1889,
he should now be removed. He wrote to Glasier, "Nothing
that I can recall has ever depressed me so much." But Hardie
was not the type to resign in a huff. He accepted a financial
payment and tributes from the ILP and was reassured that his
contributions would still be sought. His successor as editor
was Glasier. It says much for both of them that their friendship

continued. Under Glasier, circulation soon rose from 13,000 to 24,000 by 1906.

Hardie was not fully recovered and his friend William Stewart pointed out that he had been very near to death and needed a rest in a warmer climate than that of Scotland. With MacDonald, who had also been ill, he went to the Riviera and, for the first time, Hardie had to miss the ILP's annual conference.

By June he was back in action and was soon abroad again for the International Socialist meeting in Amsterdam. The debate was dominated by the issue of class warfare versus progress through democracy. Two other incidents moved Hardie. One was the public handshake between the Russian and Japanese delegates, whose countries were at war. Hardie ardently hoped that future wars could be avoided by working-class people refusing to kill each other. The other was the presence of a representative from India who criticized the rule of Britain over his country. Imperialism and its effects was increasingly a matter of concern to Hardie.

In early 1905 Hardie was invited by a prominent journalist to outline his political programme. He started by saying that society should be organized not for profit but for the benefit of all. He continued with more precise policies for abolishing poverty. He wanted decent housing for all to the standard enjoyed by the middle classes. He argued for crèches at work for women and play spaces for children. The last point indicated his growing desire for a society built around the needs of women and children. This was a personal statement, not one made on behalf of the ILP or the LRC. But that was soon to come as an election drew near.

The Conservative government resigned in December 1905, to be succeeded by the Liberals led by Campbell-Bannerman. He soon dissolved Parliament for the election of 1906.

CHAPTER 7

SOCIALIST, PARTY LEADER, TRAVELLER, 1906–1909

Hardie wrote thousands of articles, up to a hundred pamphlets, yet few books. Yet he had two books published in the space of two years, one in 1907 and one in 1909. This chapter will start with the book that contains his fullest exposition of socialism. It will end with one on India, which was one of the few early books on Labour's policy toward the Empire. In between, attention will be given to his role in Parliament, in which he now had the backing of a sizeable number of colleagues.

Hardie did not consider himself a political theorist, yet thousands of working-class people knew him as socialist and many were converted by him to that creed. In 1907, he published a short book, about 4,000 words, called *From Serfdom to Socialism*. It does not rank as an intellectual or historic masterpiece. Nonetheless, Hardie's friend William Stewart was not exaggerating when he wrote that "the charm of the book lies in its lucidity and in the complete avoidance of that technical and turgid terminology which looks scientific, but, for the ordinary reader, is only befogging".[1]

Hardie tried to explain just what he meant by socialism. It entailed public rather than private ownership of property, that is of land and capital. The reason was that property leads to power. He wrote in his book, "The economic objective of socialism is to make land and industrial capital common property, and to cease to produce for the profit of the landlord and the capitalist and to begin to produce for the use of the community."[2] The power inherent in property was concentrated in a minority, who used it for their own ends rather than the common good, and hence it had to be made public. He was not saying that private ownership would not exist, that people would not own the clothes they wore. He meant that the ownership of essential industries, large estates, and wealth which gave the few dominance over the many could only be ended by public ownership.

There was more. A socialist society was one characterized by equality. He stated: "Socialism implies the inherent equality of all human beings. It does not assume that all are alike but only that all are equal."[3] Given that all people are born of equal worth, it follows that all resources and opportunities should be distributed as equally as possible. This did not mean that every person should receive the same income, as clearly a person with a large family required more than a single person. Instead of some people receiving or owning millions of pounds while others possessed little, there should just be modest differences.

Hardie quickly made clear that socialism was not limited to the material distribution of and the public ownership of goods. He continued: "Socialism is much more than either a political creed or an economic dogma. It presents to the world a new conception of society and a new basis upon which to build up the life of the individual."[4] First, members are concerned for the common good: "To the socialist the community represents a large family organisation in which the strong should employ their gifts in promoting the wealth of all, instead of using their strength for their own personal aggrandisement."[5] Second, workers would be "productive", that is they would produce the essentials of healthy living and do so in shorter working hours, so leaving more time for family life and leisure. He regarded working at the stock exchange, for the army, and in domestic service for those of higher status as unproductive.

Not least, socialism was about peace. Thus equality was not just applied to one nation. He wrote that "the socialist applies it also to all races. Only by a full and unqualified recognition of this claim can peace be restored to the world."[6]

Hardie's socialism was essentially about equality. All people had a right to help shape a new kind of society. They could use their powers to achieve a more equal society by the public ownership of essential industries and the just redistribution of goods between individuals. This material equality would occur when members were bound to each other by a commitment to the common good. This mutuality, this caring for each other, this fraternity, was the heart of socialism. And it extended to other races and so promoted peace.

HARDIE AND MARX

From where did Hardie get his socialism? In his time, the best-known theoretical exponent of socialism was Karl Marx. In *From Serfdom to Socialism* Hardie revealed that he had read some Marx. Further, for a while he had verbal and written communication with Friedrich Engels, who succeeded Marx as the Marxist theorist. Engels, like Eleanor Marx, later criticized Hardie for rejecting revolutionary Marxism.

So was he a Marxist? Professor Kenneth Morgan answers the question. He explains that elements of Marxism did appeal to Hardie, especially the vision of a classless society. He drew attention to Marx's later claim that in some countries socialism could be achieved by a peaceful process. But he tended to ignore both Marx's economic analysis and his usual assertion that capitalism could be overthrown only by violence. Morgan concludes: "There is scant evidence that he had much first-hand acquaintance with Marx's writings."[7] My view is that Hardie read some Marx and selected bits which fitted with his own views of an ethical and peaceful socialism. In *From Serfdom to Socialism*, Hardie does recommend Marx's *Capital*, but also books by Robert Blatchford, Thomas Carlyle, John Ruskin, Henry George, and Sidney Webb, who were anything but Marxist. Certainly, the contemporary Marxists who often allied with the Socialist Democratic Foundation (SDF) tended to sneer at Hardie for his lack of Marxism.

Perhaps the key point is that almost certainly Hardie was a socialist before he read Marx. Hardie became a socialist by experience. Seeing the needless poverty of his neighbours and the sufferings of miners in a land where some dwelt in luxury convinced him that a new economic and social system was required, a system that was called socialism. He was not alone. His miner friend Bob Smillie, after seeing some miners badly injured in pit accidents for which they received no compensation and others evicted for striking for a living wage, concluded that "it was the failure of our industrial system to distribute the wealth produced equitably which caused the tremendous inequalities of our social system, and the consequent class cleavage and bitterness... It made me a Labour leader."[8]

AND THE BIBLE

One other major influence on Hardie's socialism, sometimes underplayed by biographers, was Christianity. He gives it prominence in his book, *From Serfdom to Socialism* where he starts by discussing the Sermon on the Mount, claiming that socialism "is a form of social economy very closely akin to the principles set forth in the Sermon on the Mount. Christ recognised clearly that the possession of private property came between man and his welfare both for time and eternity."[9] He was referring to Christ's injunction in Matthew 6, "Lay not up for yourselves treasures upon earth," and his warning, "Ye cannot serve God and Mammon". He also drew attention to Christ telling his disciples to follow his example and to be servants to others.

Hardie has been accused of restricting his Christianity to the New Testament: far from it. He wrote:

> The Mosaic laws for the regulation of the holding of land and the treatment of the poor and the unfortunate cannot perhaps be described as socialistic in the modern sense of the word [but]... they were quite as drastic in their way as are many of the socialist proposals of our day. Usury was prohibited, land could neither be sold outright nor held for more than a limited period as security for debt; even the debtor was freed from all obligations when the jubilee came round.[10]

Moving forward in the Old Testament, he stated that the prophets

> were loud in their denunciations of the folly of those who expected happiness from riches. They beheld the tears of the oppressed and saw that on the side of the oppressors there was wealth and power... Social equality and fierce denunciations of the rich form the staple of the writings we are now required to look upon as having been inspired... Clearly the modern system of wealth accumulation, which is rooted and grounded in land monopoly, usury, and the fleecing of the poor, finds no support in the Old Testament scriptures.[11]

Nor was he ignorant of the teachings of the early church fathers. In Hardie's day, some preachers called upon St Paul's assertion that those who would not work should not eat as a justification for harsh treatment of the unemployed. Hardie responded by calling upon St John Chrysostom's interpretation that Paul was referring to rich idlers. He continued that the poor were often idle because no work was available and added that socialists had a duty to create an environment which facilitated full employment so that those willing to work could do so.

Christianity was an early influence upon Hardie. It coincided with the period of his own face-to-face experience with poverty, suffering, and inequality. He met a Christ who sympathized with the poor rather than the rich and who urged his followers not to lord it over others but to act as their servants. They were brothers. He read of a Christ who condemned the accumulation of private wealth, in that it drove its owners to treat other people badly and also in that it endangered their own relationship with God. In the Old Testament he discovered that the ownership of property was not sacrosanct and could and should be more fairly distributed. The charging of interest on loans was forbidden. He came across God's prophets strongly attacking the rich who ignored the poor. Here was the basis of Hardie's socialism.

Hardie never said that Christianity and socialism were one and the same. He recognized that many Christians were not socialists. He welcomed unbelievers into the Labour Party. But he saw an overlap between Christianity and socialism and he believed that the teachings of Scripture and the example of Christ offered insights for building a socialist and better society. On a number of occasions, he said that Christianity was the biggest motivating factor in his life and the basis on which he built his socialism. His attitude to money, his avoidance of the company of the rich and powerful, his readiness to be alongside ordinary working-class people, and his dislike of privilege and status all derived from his understanding of Christianity. Significantly, many of his closest political associates were what can be called Christian socialists, such as Henderson, Crooks, Snowden, and Lansbury. Hardie's socialism, as *From Serfdom to Socialism* makes clear, cannot be understood without his Christianity. Hardie's Christianity thus throws light on how he formed his socialism. How was it to be attained? In the book he insisted on the vehicle of democracy. He lived in the century in which male suffrage had been widely extended. It was true that economic and social power still resided with the upper and middle classes who dominated the Conservative and Liberal parties. Nonetheless, democratic change was now possible and fitted well with Hardie's understanding of Christianity as a non-violent creed.

This democracy was to be won by the Independent Labour Party (ILP). Even before it gained a substantial number of seats in the Commons, socialists and Labourites were winning places as local councillors and planning a municipal socialism which was to be expressed in the form of local authorities taking gas, electricity, and other services into public hands and away from private ownership.

The chief goal, though, was the Labour Party making progress in central government. The party would consist of both socialists and non-socialists, and would include some middle-class members, but its heart was to be the working class. Hardie wrote: "But it is to the working-class itself that we must look for changing the system."[12] The working class could provide the votes to win an election and the able working-class MPs who knew at first hand the needs of their constituents.

Not just the Labour Party: trade unions had a major role to play in persuading employers to improve working conditions. Hardie recognized that the co-operative movement was important in bringing working-class people together in joint ventures. Unlike many socialist writers, in this book Hardie also acknowledged that socialism, like Christianity, required followers who lived out their beliefs in individual practice. Brotherhood, co-operation, peace, and self-sacrifice were more than slogans; they were virtues to be expressed in everyday life. For Hardie, socialism was both structural and personal. It required structural changes to bring about public ownership and it also required personal characteristics which attracted others to socialism.

Hardie must have been writing his book during 1906. It was remarkable how he found the time in a year which had two general elections. At least he had a handbook from which he could expound his beliefs. He was a practitioner, not just a writer.

RETAINS HIS SEAT IN 1906 ELECTION

At the end of 1905, the faltering Conservative government split over the question of protectionism or free trade. The Liberals took over and in January 1906 their new leader, Sir Henry Campbell-Bannerman – an elderly and shrewd Scot – called a general election. Hardie flung himself into his favourite role of Labour evangelist and in three days travelled 1,120 miles to address seven meetings.

Hardie was careful, however, not to repeat his mistake of neglecting his own Merthyr constituency. Dai Davies and other members of the Merthyr Trades Council had kept his local organization in place, while Frank Smith and Emmeline Pankhurst were soon there to help. Moreover, Lillie was constantly by his side. His programme was a radical one that included abolition of the House of Lords, women's suffrage, old-age pensions, and disestablishment of the state church in Wales. His socialism was made clear in his demand that basic industries should pass from private to public ownership.

Some commentators claim that Hardie had lost the support

of nonconformists on three grounds. First, that he had not responded to the many requests from Welsh chapels for financial donations. Second, that he had insufficiently opposed the Education Act (1902), which had given financial backing to Church of England schools, enabling them to convey their teaching with state money. Third, that he had shown little enthusiasm for the Welsh revival of 1904, which had converted many miners to Christianity and away from drink.

The criticisms had some truth but Hardie rebuffed them. He simply could not afford to give to a host of churches. He did oppose the Education Act but not so much because he was a nonconformist. Rather he was uneasy about the teaching of religion in schools. He welcomed the conversions made at the revival but expressed doubts as to whether its sheer emotionalism would soon fade within individuals.

The important point is that these criticisms did not, in fact, seem to dent his popularity with church people. Although the Welsh revival received much publicity, less has been given to what was called "the New Theology", which attracted many nonconformists, including Hardie himself. One of its leading exponents was the Reverend R. J. Campbell, the minister of the City Temple in London (not far from the accommodation into which Hardie moved). In an interview lodged with the Cumnock archives, Fenner Brockway emphasizes the importance of religion to Hardie and states that he had a close association with the journal edited by Campbell called *The Christian Commonwealth*. The New Theology was never a church, it was rather an approach which gave attention to social as well as spiritual issues and which contested the hold many wealthy industrialists had on nonconformist churches. In the constituency, these kinds of ministers supported Hardie.

When the Merthyr results were declared, Hardie with 10,187 was a convincing second to D. A. Thomas and was so elected again.

Overall, the Liberals were the winners. They secured 377 seats, giving them an overall majority of 84 over all the other parties. Campbell-Bannerman soon appointed some talented ministers, with Herbert Asquith as chancellor of the exchequer, Herbert Gladstone as home secretary, and the rising David Lloyd George, who had attended a Welsh elementary school, as president of the Board of Trade. John Burns finally ended his flirtation with Labour and became president of the local government board.

The Labour Representation Committee (LRC) also had cause to rejoice. It had put up 50 candidates and 29 gained seats. As Iain McLean observed, it was "a triumphant vindication of Hardie and the principle of independent Labour representation".[13] In addition, the MacDonald–Gladstone pact was vital in allowing some of its candidates to stand without Liberal opposition. MacDonald was one of the new MPs along with Philip Snowden, both of whom were to hold high office in future Labour governments. The LRC now became known as the Labour Party. Financial and organizational support still came from the ILP and trade unions but it was the MPs who decided its program.

LEADER OF THE LABOUR PARTY

These Labour MPs agreed to elect a leader on a yearly basis. Hardie might have seemed the obvious choice, but not so. The Labour MPs certainly respected him as a founder of the party but they were not sure that he would be the best leader in the Commons. David Shackleton, who had impressed in his three years as an MP, allowed his name to go forward. He appealed to those who did not want the party too closely associated with socialism. The ballot ended in a tie. In a second one, Hardie won fifteen to fourteen, that is by one vote. Apparently, MacDonald had abstained in the first ballot and voted for

Hardie in the second. Narrow margin or not, Hardie was the first elected leader of the Parliamentary Labour Party (the PLP). MacDonald became secretary and Henderson chief whip.

Biographers of Hardie have tended to criticize his parliamentary leadership. They point out that he was bored by committee meetings and that his direct speaking style was not a success in parliamentary debates. Yet, as Morgan explains, the PLP held together and "made a significant impact".[14] The Labour Party supported the government's Education Bill, with Hardie backing an amendment to eliminate the teaching of sectarian doctrines in schools financed by public money. The bill was rejected in the Lords, which lent weight to his campaign in the election that the House of Lords should be abolished.

Even more important, Labour scored an astonishing victory in the Taff Vale case. The Liberal government produced a bill which failed to give trade unions full immunity when sued by employers for damages following strikes and picketing. Labour then produced its own bill, for which Shackleton did most of the detailed preparation. Hardie led its verbal presentation and cleverly quoted from a number of Liberal candidates, including Asquith, who, in their manifestos, had promised immunity in order to win working-class votes. Remarkably Campbell-Bannerman rose and announced Liberal support for Labour's proposals. Even more remarkably it passed the Lords, who were concentrating on fighting other legislation.

The Labour Party could not outvote the government, yet it had caused it to drop its traditional support for individual factory-owners in favour of collective action by trade unions. And the latter were appreciative, with even more moving to Labour. The old tie between trade unions and the Liberal Party if not completely broken was undermined. As W. Knox explains, "the shift of the unions towards Labour was based on expediency rather than ideology".[15] If Hardie had attempted to limit membership of the Labour Party to socialist bodies or if he had been an out and out Marxist, this shift would not have occurred.

Within the Commons, the party continued to keep social welfare matters on the agenda. In 1906 it got through a bill to enable local authorities to provide school meals to needy pupils. It was making the important point that schools had a social as well as an educational role. Hardie frequently returned to his old concern with unemployment. As chair of the party, Hardie served on the Select Committee on Income Tax. Drawing upon the work of Snowden, who had become the party's tax expert, he submitted a memorandum which argued that unearned income should be taxed more heavily than earned. His arguments may well have influenced Asquith's budget of 1907, which included graduated income tax and slightly increased death duties in the highest ranges.

On 24 October 1906 Hardie's fiftieth birthday was celebrated at the Memorial Hall. He received 447 telegrams of congratulations. He was presented with a gold watch and Lillie with a gold-topped umbrella. Hardie, it was reported, thanked the audience for honouring his wife, who "had borne so well the toil of his home and so often his long separation from her and the children".

While Hardie chaired it, the party was more significant than its parliamentary size warranted. Yet just at this time his leadership came under more fire. One reason was his attitude toward the movement for women's suffrage.

WOMEN'S SUFFRAGE

During the nineteenth century, women gained the vote in local elections and the right to sit on school boards and boards of poor law guardians and, in 1907, on local councils. Yet they were still denied the vote in parliamentary elections. Pressure for change came from two main organizations. The moderate

National Union of Women's Suffrage Societies (the NUWSS) had been formed in 1867 and was led by Millicent Fawcett. More militant suffragettes belonged to the Women's Social and Political Union (the WSPU) founded in 1903 by Mrs Emmeline Pankhurst and her daughters Christabel and Sylvia.

The movements were split not just on methodology but also on strategy. The NUWSS sought the enfranchisement of all women. Many ILP members favoured this in the belief that it would encompass working-class women who would vote Labour. The WSPU aimed immediately for enfranchisement on the same terms as men – which still excluded the poorest. They argued that such a change could be brought about quickly by a straightforward act, which would avoid the complications of whether the position of men would also have to be changed.

Hardie had a long record of supporting the political and social advancement of women. As early as the Mid Lanark campaign he was calling for votes for women. He condemned the low wages of those who worked, helped those who wanted trade union activity, and was one of the first politicians to want state day nurseries to enable more women to work. Surprisingly, he backed the aim of the WSPU for limited suffrage, rather than the enfranchisement of all men and women. His justification was strategic. The powerful Asquith was an opponent of votes for women. The steadfast and astute Arthur Henderson acknowledged that "there was no practical possibility" of a universal bill and, at most, "what could be got was a limited one, extending the vote to certain categories of women".[16] Hardie also drew upon surveys which showed that, although the WSPU was organized by middle-class women, of those likely to receive the vote under a limited act, 80 per cent would be working class.

What annoyed Hardie's colleagues, and was seized upon by his enemies, was that the cause of women seemed to become all-important to him. This was attributed to the strong influence

Emmeline Pankhurst now had on him. He sympathized with the militant, disruptive tactics adopted by the WSPU and openly welcomed Christabel Pankhurst and Annie Kenney on their release from prison in 1905. His support continued even after Mrs Pankhurst publicly criticized, and then left, the Labour Party for its lack of commitment to the WSPU. Hardie was not the only member of the Labour Party to side with the WSPU. George Lansbury did so and was also close to the Pankhursts. But Lansbury was not yet an MP, let alone party leader.

Not so well known at this stage was Hardie's growing friendship with Sylvia Pankhurst after she became a student at the Royal College of Art. Sylvia, initially with her brother Harry, sometimes visited Hardie and he took her under his wing. When she was later imprisoned, Hardie frequently raised her case in the Commons. Fenner Brockway, who knew Hardie well, makes clear that it was not Sylvia but Emmeline who won Hardie's political admiration. Nonetheless, his friendship with this young woman was likely to inflame the feeling that he was emotionally attached to the female militants.

In 1907, the Labour Party conference was in Belfast, where a proposal in support of limited suffrage was heavily defeated. Hardie then declared that if the vote was intended to limit his actions as an MP in the Commons, "I shall have to seriously consider whether I shall remain a member of the Parliamentary Party." The background to this struggle was not just the women's issue. A number of socialists, led by Ben Tillett, were arguing that MPs were simply delegates who carried out the wishes of members, presumably of the ILP. Hardie and his fellow MPs were opposed to this, saying, first, that they were elected by constituents not members and, secondly, that they as MPs had to choose how to vote. Hardie did not resign and soon the PLP again elected him as its leader.

The rise and fall of Victor Grayson

Hardie was in a curious position. His popularity meant that his threat to resign prompted dismay. Yet concern over his apparent obsession with the WSPU, combined with a section of the party which regarded him as too soft a socialist, did make him vulnerable. It came to a head in the person of a new figure, Victor Grayson. Having abandoned studies to be a Unitarian minister, the 25-year-old Grayson had been invited by the Labour League – which was not affiliated to the ILP – in the Colne Valley to stand as their candidate. Suddenly, a by-election became due when the sitting MP was elevated to the Lords and Grayson was elected as a socialist MP by a margin of 153 votes. He immediately attacked the ILP for compromising with what he regarded as conservative trade unions. This implied a criticism of Hardie, who, after years of rebuffs from the TUC, had been greeted with rapturous applause at its 1907 conference.

But Hardie had fallen ill. In February 1907 he had suffered a chronic inflammation of the bowels and may also have had a mild stroke. In April, he underwent an operation to remove the bowel obstruction and, under medical orders to rest, retreated to the Wemyss Bay Hydropathic Centre. Resting with the Scottish middle classes in luxurious surroundings did not suit him and he opted for a world tour, during which he could both rest and meet other working-class politicians. The radical Joseph Fels, a Jewish American who made a fortune in soap manufacture, financed him and in July Hardie sailed for Canada.

The details of his world tour, culminating in his book on India, will be brought together at the end of this chapter. For the sake of continuity in Britain, his activities in the Commons will now be picked up from his return in May 1908.

Hardie was welcomed back at a packed Albert Hall, where

he had to wait ten minutes before the cheering subsided to let him speak. Working-class supporters still regarded him as their leader, although the undercurrents of criticisms continued.

Politics had changed, in that Campbell-Bannerman had died and been replaced by Asquith, with Lloyd George as chancellor of the exchequer. The Liberals had decided to extend their social welfare appeal. Hardie too had changed. He appeared to have realized that he had been too close to the WSPU, although as explained by Professor Mary Davis, historian of the women's movements, "Hardie himself must take much of the credit" for the support given to the suffrage drive by Labour.[17] Henderson had taken over from Hardie as leader of the PLP but had found it difficult to do much except offer encouragement to the Liberal government. Hardie determined on a more vigorous intervention and attacked Edward VII for a visit, approved by the Liberals, to the despotic Tsar of Russia. In response, the angry king refused to include Hardie in an invitation to MPs to a reception at Windsor.

Next he pressed the government to implement and extend the Unemployed Workmen's Act (1905) so that local authorities rather than voluntary bodies took the main responsibility. John Burns, now president of the Local Government Board, enjoyed declining to act.

The Liberals had other plans to win working-class votes. The budget of 1908, mainly devised by Asquith, introduced a non-contributory old-age pension. A mere 5s. a week, it was only for those aged seventy and over whose weekly income was below 10s: a small start but the beginning of state pensions. After a struggle, the Lords let it through.

Meanwhile, Victor Grayson was leading the attack on Hardie and the Labour Party, accusing them of doing nothing about unemployment. On 15 October, after a confrontation with the Speaker, he was led out of the chamber yelling to the Labour

MPs, "You are traitors to your class." The following day, after another confrontation, he screamed, "This house is a house of murderers." His antics may have pleased the minority of left-wing socialists who considered Hardie a compromiser but soon Grayson went too far when he – and Hyndman – refused to speak on the same platform as Hardie. He thus insulted "the grand old man", as Hardie was beginning to be called, and identified himself with the SDF rather than the ILP.

In fact, Hardie was active on unemployment both within and without the Commons. He tried to pass legislation to finance local authorities to set up labour bureaux and to pay the wages for new employment schemes. He was active in the Joint London Right to Work Committee, wrote strong articles and addressed numerous meetings. The year ended with the passing of the Miners' Eight Hours Bill (although it was later modified by the Lords). Hardie recalled that, twenty-two years before, he had sat in the Commons' gallery when it was talked out. He now rejoiced, "I voted in the majority for the third reading of the bill."

The following year, Grayson raised his head again. At the ILP conference in Edinburgh in April 1909, Hardie strongly defended the record of the PLP and won a huge majority against a motion to pay Grayson a parliamentary salary even though he refused to sign the constitution. Surprisingly, Grayson then won an amendment that reference to his refusal to speak with Hardie be deleted from the records. Hardie, MacDonald, and Glasier (whose editorship of the *Labour Leader* had been unjustly savaged by Grayson) promptly resigned from the National Administrative Council (the NAC), that is the executive of the ILP. Later Snowden joined them. They were worried about Grayson's disruptive tactics, his undermining of the alliance between the ILP and trade unions, and his agreement with Blatchford that militarism should be backed. It was time for a showdown and the canny Hardie knew what

SOCIALIST, PARTY LEADER, TRAVELLER, 1906–1909

he was doing. Conference was dismayed: after all Hardie had been a member since its inauguration. Trade unions were opposed to Grayson. The ILP's membership declined. Before long the new NAC denounced Grayson. His day was over and even the electors in Colne Valley left him.

Dealing with Grayson was one thing, dealing with the new Liberals was another. In 1909, Lloyd George presented his "people's budget" with the backing of Labour, now chaired by George Barnes. Lloyd George had borrowed Labour ideas, particularly those circulated by Philip Snowden. Not that Lloyd George mentioned this when he introduced the first tax on petrol, increased duty on spirits, raised income tax with a supertax of 6d. in the pound on incomes over £5,000, and introduced children's allowances for tax payers earning under £500 and certain land taxes. It allocated £100,000 to found a system of labour exchanges. Money had to be raised to pay for more battleships as well as social services. Labour was in a tricky position. It could be credited with creating the political conditions under which the Liberals felt compelled to promote social welfare reforms. But the Liberals looked likely to reap the votes.

Further, a ruling in the High Court in the Osborne case had cast doubts on the legality of the political levy which trade unions imposed on members and which contributed to their financial support of the Labour Party. In order to get this overturned, Labour had to work in conjunction with the Liberals.

In November 1909 the Lords rejected the budget and Asquith dissolved Parliament in protest. The parties prepared for "the peers versus the people" election of January 1910. Labour's problem was how to appear more than just an appendage to the Liberals.

World tour and India

This chapter will now return to Hardie's world tour and his subsequent book on India. In July 1907 he sailed to Canada. He wrote for the *Labour Leader* that emigration to Canada was unlikely to solve the problems of Britain's unemployed, as jobs were just as hard to find there. It is worth noting that in 1908, accompanied by Lillie and Nan, and again in 1912, Hardie returned briefly to Canada when he encouraged trade unions and political Labourites to draw together. In 1907, he sailed from Canada's Pacific coast for a short stay in Japan and then landed in India.

Hardie already had a reputation as an internationalist. This had derived mainly from his interest in Europe and the USA. Apart from his opposition to the government's Boer War, he had had little to do with the Empire. This now changed as he set foot in Calcutta.

India was going through a difficult period under the British viceroy, Lord Curzon. He had divided the province of Bengal and created a new province of East Bengal. As it had a large majority of Muslims, Hindus saw it as an attempt to weaken them. Pressure for change was stimulated by the Hindu-majority Indian National Congress movement, which had two elements, one later led by the young lawyer Mahatama Gandhi, with a constitutional, non-violent philosophy, and one by the more militant B. G. Tilak. Some violence did occur but much more widespread were boycotts of European goods and demands for home rule.

Soon the British press, especially *The Times*, was accusing Hardie of encouraging sedition, terrorism, and revolution. Edward VII wrote to Curzon, "What can one expect if such a scoundrel as Keir Hardie... ferments sedition in India and at home against our mode of government?"

In fact, the reports were wilful misrepresentations of what

Hardie said. The journalist who had sent them was challenged to produce his evidence and could not do so. But the damage was done. What Hardie saw and wrote will be shown in the section devoted to his book.

From India, Hardie went to Australia, where he resumed contact with Tom Mann and with the first Labour prime minister, not only in Australia but in the world. This was Andrew Fisher, whom Hardie had known as an Ayrshire miner. In New Zealand, Hardie applauded the eight-hour day and old-age pensions but feared that the Labour movement was too close to the Liberals.

Finally he went to South Africa. He was already aware of cruel white discrimination against black people and had condemned it in the Commons. Those who accompanied him advised Hardie to steer clear of racial issues. They might just as well have advised him to take a seat in the House of Lords. At Durban, his proposal to open trade unions to every person regardless of race provoked fierce opposition. Thereafter, at every station at which his trains stopped, crowds gathered to jeer and threaten him. He wrote wryly: "Many of these were Boer farmers who had already forgotten the stand I had made on their behalf and for which I had been stoned and hunted throughout the towns and cities in both England and Scotland." At a final meeting in Johannesburg, he spoke no more than a few sentences before a riot ensued from which he just escaped with his life, clutching a tattered Union Flag which he later pinned up in Neville's Court as a reminder.

Back in Britain in May 1908, Hardie questioned the self-satisfaction of politicians – including that of the Liberals – with progress in South Africa. He was one of the very few to condemn publicly the treatment of black people there.

BOOK ON INDIA

India remained his prime concern, as expressed in his widely read *India: Impressions and Suggestions*, published in 1909. Caroline Benn calls it no more than "a pamphlet".[18] It contains 126 pages of cogent argument and is probably his best book. *India* is partly drawn from articles he sent back to the *Labour Leader* as he travelled through India and contains some of the descriptions of people, animals, and scenery at which he excelled.

More importantly, he draws upon conversations with a wide range of Indians. He did not seek out high officials, although he met some. He did spend time with some "Indian gentlemen", as he called them, but also with traders, peasant farmers, and poor labourers. In one modest hotel, he woke to find nearby a man and a snake dead together. Apparently, the man had been bitten by the snake yet managed to kill it before he too succumbed. Hardie mixed with a range of people drawn from different religions, races, and classes and, unusually for books about the Empire, gave much space to the views of those who were rarely if ever consulted by white people.

Impressions drawn from human contact were bolstered by statistics, often taken from official sources. He proves his assertion that talented Indians were kept from higher positions in the civil service by publishing the government's own tables, which revealed that only sixteen Indians were in the best paid posts in the administrative section, only six in education, and none in the customs.

Not least, Hardie wrote from a deep respect for India. He points out that its civilizations blossomed many years before those in Britain, especially in regard to education, art, science, religion, and literature. Yet, he continued, "our whole system of government in India rests upon the assumption that its people are either unfit or unworthy to be trusted with even the semblance of self-government".[19] His journalistic ability to observe, a readiness to listen to people of all ranks, his detailed grasp of statistics, his skill in analysing problems, and his respect for Indians, led to a powerful, passionate, and purposeful publication.

Hardie witnessed widespread suffering and death. During 1908 failed harvests and rising food prices led to famine conditions which affected 49 million people. Poverty was accompanied by plague, which cost 1 million lives that year. In the village of Chaybopore, he described gaunt faces, and bodies so thin that ribs were visible. Death was accepted. Hardie was amazed that starving parents valued schooling so much that they put their children's small school fees before food. Despite the death toll, the government refused to reduce taxes. It angered Hardie that these went partly toward a rapidly growing military budget.

Officials shrugged that India had always had famine and starvation. Hardie disagreed. Before British rule, Indian rulers had taken a quarter of the crop of small farmers. In a bad year, when the yield was small, the tax in kind dropped proportionately. Britain insisted that taxes were paid in cash, with no drop in bad years. Moreover, the peasants had previously cut wood down for free fuel and fished for free food. Now they had to pay. He cited the viceroy's own figures that the annual average income in India was £2 (compared with £42 in Britain), with many far below the average. The poorest found themselves in the hands of loan sharks. Hardie summed up that there "is abundant evidence to justify the belief that the condition of the Indian peasant has worsened under British rule".[20]

A long-time opponent of racism, in India he called it "the colour line". He cited many examples told to him about how Indians were humiliated by the white British. A prosperous Indian Christian was joined in a railway compartment by his son, who was darker in complexion than his father. White passengers objected and one military officer snarled, "We tolerated you [the father] because you don't look so bad, but I'll be damned if we allow that black dog beside us." Then Hardie saw it himself. In East Bengal, he arranged to visit a prison and was accompanied by a number of Indians, including Jagesh Chowdhury, an Oxford-educated barrister. A white magistrate appeared to let Hardie in and immediately shouted at the Indians to leave. When Chowdhury explained who he was, the angry abuse became even louder. The Indians, with dignity, walked away. Hardie remained – in order to give the magistrate a tongue-lashing – and then joined them. Hardie acknowledged that this might have been an extreme instance but added that the prevailing mood of the British Raj was that all Indians had to be kept in their place.

The nominal capital was Calcutta but for eight months of the year the highest British rulers retreated to Simla, some seven thousand feet above sea level, where the air was pure and the temperature moderate. Meanwhile, many Indians were dying in the sweltering heat. This physical distance, Hardie explained, was akin to the social distance between the races. The senior officials, he accepted, might have been educated, even enlightened, men but the gulf between them and the Indians meant that they never understood or appreciated them. Significantly, the viceroy had no Indian secretary or senior adviser. There was a legislative council to assist the viceroy which included some elected members but they could not present a bill without the viceroy's permission. Provincial bodies included Indians but they possessed few powers and were in the hands of white civil servants.

He did not call for the immediate withdrawal of the British but argued for a different form of government, writing: "the people of India are fit to be trusted with such a large measure of self-government as would give them effective control over their own affairs and generally reduce British interference to the same limits as are exercised over the colonies in Australia or South Africa".[21]

This would entail Indians being at the highest levels of leadership and administration. It would mean that councils at all levels would have powers over policies and budgets. Hardie then penned the noble words: "When Indian can meet European as a fully enfranchised equal, and compel that respect which is his due, then, and not before, will race prejudice begin to die out and finally to disappear."[22]

The Indians gave Hardie a reception to mark his departure. He was moved when the band played "My love she's but a lassie yet." He finished, "I went to India to see the people and to learn of their grievances; during the two months I was there I mixed with the people, companioned with them, and found them sociable, trustworthy, and lovable. Their ability is not open to question."[23]

Once published, Hardie's book had a strong influence on politicians and the public. Few Labour MPs had shown an interest in the Empire but now they formed a definite policy toward it. And not just Labour: Morgan records that the volume "played a major role in educating British Liberal opinion on Indian affairs".[24] Writing of Britain after the Second World War, Morgan continued that both Labour and Conservative governments "engaged in colonial liberation, as Hardie had so long demanded, against such overwhelming odds".[25]

Within the Commons, Hardie thereafter frequently spoke on Indian affairs with speeches notable for up-to-date information gained from his Indian friends. He attacked the heavy taxes imposed on Indians, condemned the heavy-handed police methods along with unjust treatment of Indians, and repeated his proposals for more democratic legislatures. After B. G. Tilak was imprisoned for six years for sedition in 1908, following a trial in which the jury consisted largely of Europeans and no

Hindus, Hardie pressed strongly for his release. The Indian rulers and the British government refused. But Hardie's influence was more long term. His visit to India and his subsequent book brought India to the attention of Parliament as never before.

CHAPTER 8

CLASS WAR AND WORLD
WAR, 1910–1915

The years 1910–1915 were marked by elections, industrial strife, the outbreak of war, and the death of Keir Hardie. Before discussing them it is time to consider Hardie's friendship with Sylvia Pankhurst. Caroline Benn says: "During 1910, Hardie's relationship with Sylvia was at its closest point."[1] Kenneth Morgan adds that "by 1911 they were passionately involved in a relationship which clearly had its physical side".[2] Fred Reid says he was "probably Sylvia Pankhurst's lover in the fullest sense".[3]

It seems astonishing that anyone – even fifty years after his death – should accuse Hardie of having an affair. He was so puritanical that he would walk away from company that made a smutty joke. When Tom Mann was a successful general secretary of the Independent Labour Party (ILP) in 1897, he left his wife and openly consorted with other women. Hardie, as party chair, sorrowfully asked him to leave. Eventually Mann emigrated to Australia. If Hardie did have an affair then he was an almighty hypocrite – although even his enemies never threw that stone at him.

Women were attracted to Hardie and he enjoyed their attention: nothing unusual in that. Once the young Sylvia came to London, Hardie welcomed her and her brother. After all, he had been a good friend of their late father and her mother. She would visit Hardie at Neville's Court, sometimes while Frank Smith or Fenner Brockway was there. They would walk along the Thames Embankment talking about socialism and votes for women.

The evidence of a possible affair rests on letters (released much later) between Sylvia and Hardie, most from Sylvia. They corresponded particularly while she was on lecture tours abroad or in prison for her suffragette activities. Of course the prison letters would have been opened by officials. Sylvia often wrote very affectionate letters, including love poetry. As Benn notes, Hardie's responses "were short and down to earth", although in one he writes about a kiss by transference (a subject she had raised) and sometimes called her "sweetie".[4] Travelling to the USA, she accepted an invitation to the cabin of the ship's doctor from which she had to make an escape. She wrote to Hardie that she had not realized how dangerous "old buffers" could be: something not very complimentary to the aging Hardie if they were in a physical relationship.

Benn finally concludes that the evidence is not sufficient to decide either way. My view is that probably there was not a sexual relationship between them for several reasons. First, Hardie never hid his friendship with Sylvia. Occasionally, he went to the theatre with Sylvia and Frank Smith. Smith, of course, was a former Salvation Army officer with similar religious and moral views to Hardie. It is hardly likely that he would have accompanied them if he considered them to be lovers. Again, Hardie openly spoke in the defence of Sylvia in the Commons following her ill-treatment in prison. No MPs made sneering innuendoes about their relationship.

Second, the people closest to him – who also knew or knew

about Sylvia – never accused him of an affair. During this period his own daughter Nan was often with him in London, helping with his correspondence. She trusted him. Looking back, years after her father's death, she regretted that her father had been unable to send her mother much money for the family, but never complained that he spent money on another woman. Nan married Emrys Hughes, who was much under Hardie's influence in the years before the war. Hughes later wrote extensively about Hardie with no mention of an affair with Sylvia.

Bruce Glasier was not part of the family but he was a staunch and intimate Labour colleague. In letters and notes, Glasier made many admiring comments about his leader. He could also be critical, especially about Hardie's promotion of himself at meetings and about what Glasier considered his misguided enthusiasm for the Women's Social and Political Union (WSPU). If an affair had existed, Glasier might not have made it public but, almost certainly, he would have written some caustic comments.

Third, his enemies did not throw mud at him about Sylvia. This was an age when the press did not mention lovers taken by royalty or senior government politicians. However, when the Irish MP and leader Charles Stewart Parnell had an extra-marital affair, he was hounded from public life.

Given the opportunity, the press would have exposed Hardie. When his electoral opponents at Merthyr accused him of supporting atheism and free love, they would have loved smears about Sylvia. But they lacked anything specific. Tom Mann returned during this decade, having left Britain when Hardie prompted him to resign from the ILP because of his sexual failings. Now they clashed vehemently when Mann accused him of failing socialism and the working class. Yet Mann never accused him of an affair.

Not least, the years in which Hardie is supposed to have been closest to Sylvia were also the ones in which Lillie saw much more of him. With the boys in work, she often accompanied him to ILP conferences and meetings, sometimes came to London, and participated in his electoral campaigns. Hardie and Lillie also went on more holidays: hardly the behaviour of a wife who suspected him of an extra-marital affair.

THE NATURE OF THEIR RELATIONSHIP

Yet there was a friendship between Keir Hardie and Sylvia Pankhurst. What was its nature? Sylvia had an unhappy childhood. Her beloved father died when she was sixteen in 1898, when she was alone in the house with him. Later her two brothers died, so that out of the family of seven, four women were left. Her mother always favoured the eldest daughter, Christabel, and Sylvia felt rejected. She needed relationships, especially with older men. Sylvia first met Hardie in her home in 1895 and wrote that her impression was of a man with "the strength of a rock, the sheltering kindness of an oak and the gentleness of a St Bernard dog".[5]

Hardie too had a difficult if very different childhood. Indeed he said he had no childhood at all, as he looked after his siblings and went to work from an early age. Benn argues that this left him with "a gloom" and that "the only time it seemed to lift was when he was with his own children, briefly, or with young women" and with Sylvia he was reconstructing "the lost play of childhood... the teasing, the games, the secrets and nonsense".[6]

In fact, Hardie was not all gloom and enjoyed social occasions throughout his life. But he did favour a kind of playfulness with Sylvia that was a break from the financial anxieties, the separation from his family, and his overwhelming workload. Some copies of letters written by Hardie to Annie Hines in 1893 are lodged at the Cumnock archives. Annie was the 21-year-old daughter of a socialist chimney sweep in Oxford. She too was a strong socialist, sometimes went for walks with Hardie and they exchanged teasing letters which she probably took more seriously than he did. Benn suggests that he "wanted her to regard him as a father or an older brother".[7]

Before leaving Sylvia, it is worth noting that after Hardie she had a friendship with the much older George Lansbury, who supported her suffrage drives, while she identified with his socialism. No one ever suggested an affair between them. Much later she devoted twenty-five years of her life to the cause of Ethiopia. Her biographer, Patricia Romero, believes that Emperor Haile Selassie was another of her father or grandfather figures. However, a more recent biographer, Mary Davis, points out that Sylvia "had not met the Emperor when she decided to take up the Ethiopian cause".[8]

Sylvia did have a baby in 1927 by Silvio Corio, an Italian who had children by other women and was no father figure. She made no secret of this. Sylvia lived until 1960, long after Hardie's close relatives were dead, and, if he had been her lover, she could have revealed it without hurting anyone. She never did. Even Morgan acknowledged: "For the rest of her life, she was haunted by the memory of Hardie as a pure, brave, uncorrupted champion of human freedom and of women's rights."[9]

Finally, it must be said that Hardie did accept offers from a number of women to help him with his correspondence, filing, and travel arrangements. Rose Davies, Agnes Hughes (sister of Emrys), and Maggie Symons were three who gave of their time. They were socialists who admired him. But they received little financial reward. It could be said that Hardie exploited them. It could also be said that Hardie was exploited by the Labour movement. Noticeably, even after they left Hardie, all continued as active and then prominent socialists.

GENERAL ELECTION OF 1910

Hardie needed all the help he could get, as January 1910 brought a general election. He was better prepared than on previous elections. He had launched a political paper in the constituency, the *Merthyr Pioneer*, with funds coming from shares sold to supporters. He and Lillie had spent a good deal of time in the constituency attending ILP and Welsh cultural gatherings. They stayed with local families and Lillie formed a friendship with the Price family, with whom she subsequently corresponded regularly.

Hardie had got on well with the other Merthyr MP, the Liberal D. A. Thomas, but he had shifted to another constituency. Pritchard Morgan, one of the Liberal candidates, and the Anti-Socialist League made vicious attacks on Hardie. Nan, who was present with Lillie and brother Jamie, recorded that their leaflets and speeches denounced him "as an advocate of atheism and free love, while questions were put to him about his country mansion in Scotland and the retinue of servants… the retinue of servants, my mother and myself, being on the platform at the time".[10] Hardie promptly published his current accounts showing a yearly income of £210, his largest ever, of which £120 was spent on his work while £90 was for food and clothes for Lillie, Nan, and himself.

He met the Anti-Socialist League head-on by proclaiming that only socialism could abolish poverty. In one talk, reported in the local paper, he said: "Poverty can never be remedied by charity, but only by justice. So long as land and industrial capital is privately owned and used to exploit the working class there is bound to be poverty. The Labour Party stands for something which no other party does. Its aim is the abolition of poverty."

Many church leaders and their followers were behind Hardie. Ministers defended him against the attacks. John James, the vice-president of the evangelical Christian Endeavour in Wales, pleaded, "Let us vote for Mr J. Keir Hardie and practical Christianity." Dr Fairbairn, late of Mansfield College, Oxford, addressing a ministers' gathering declared, "I know him intimately... seldom in my life have I met a more deeply religious man." Nan was moved by an article by Canon Adderly in *The Christian Commonwealth*, in which he "wondered at the meekness with which he [Hardie] met the foul attacks made by his Liberal opponent".

The Christian vote, with its growing emphasis on social reform, was by now an important part of Hardie's support. The attacks by the Liberals and the Anti-Socialist League backfired, as they were shown to be no more than lies. Hardie easily defeated Pritchard Morgan and increased his vote by over 3,000. Noticeably, his emphasis on the need for socialism increased rather than decreased his support.

Elsewhere Labour lost four seats, including that of Victor Grayson, but increased its numbers to forty-two, as the mining unions were now affiliated to the Labour Party along with their MPs. The increase was welcome, although Hardie was concerned that more of the MPs were Labour without being socialist. But the party was growing. Hardie announced in a speech at Newport that ten years ago affiliated membership of the Labour Party (or its equivalent) had been 375,931; now it was 1,418,868. Then it had two MPs; now over 40. Overall, the Liberals had 275 seats, Conservatives 273, Irish Nationalists 82 and Labour 42. The Liberal government would depend upon the backing of the minority parties.

George Barnes, the leader of the Parliamentary Labour Party, a long-time friend of Hardie, proved unadventurous. Mindful that only the government could reverse the Osborne judgment, he sided with the government's view that if a measure passed the Commons three times in consecutive sessions then it became law even if defeated in the Lords. Hardie was still worried by a minority of socialists who considered the party ineffective and he voiced support for the abolition of the Lords. However, in April 1910 the Lords passed what was in essence the 1909 budget and the crisis was postponed.

Hardie's Christianity did not decline in his final years. Nor was it something he just called on during elections. In May he was at Lille, in France, to speak for the National Council of the Pleasant Sunday Afternoon movement. Also known as the Brotherhood, particularly at F. B. Meyer's church in Lambeth, it drew in working-class men. Hardie attracted such a crowd to the meeting, 6,000 had to listen outside in the public square. He did not disappoint them with his usual blend of Christianity and socialism. He repeated a statement he made more than once, "I myself have found in the Christianity of Christ the inspiration which first of all drove me into the movement and has carried me on in it."

In the same month, Edward VII died suddenly and his eldest son succeeded as George V. In the Commons, Hardie quickly moved changes to the civil list to delete allowances to the king's sons and daughters. His amendment did not even obtain the backing of all Labour MPs, for not all shared his republicanism.

The major parties could not agree on a plan to reform the Lords. The Liberal government took the opportunity to persuade the new king to agree to appoint many new peers, if the Liberals were elected again, to allow its reductions of the Lords' powers to go through. The second general election of 1910 thus took place in December. Hardie easily held on to his seat. Despite putting up fewer candidates, because of a lack of money, the Labour Party increased its numbers by two. Hardie was particularly pleased at the election of George Lansbury for Bow and Bromley. An out and out socialist, he was also a pacifist and a supporter of Sylvia Pankhurst.

The Labour MPs soon elected MacDonald as their leader.

He and Hardie had had a long relationship in which they both admired and disliked each other. Hardie acknowledged MacDonald's skills as an administrator, organizer, and parliamentary speaker. He disliked his enjoyment of the company of establishment figures and his distance from working-class people and doubted his real commitment to socialism. MacDonald recognized Hardie as the major founder of the Labour Party and as an outstanding speaker to working-class audiences – even if he was jealous that Hardie always seemed to be in the limelight. He criticized his lack of stability as an MP and his weakness in forming strategy. In 1910, MacDonald gave priority to parliamentary procedure, to obtaining payment for MPs – achieved in 1911 – and to the reversal of the Osborne decision. His priorities were for Labour to be effective in the Commons and work with the Liberals. Hardie wanted a party that was effective in the country.

The overall result of the December election was that Liberals and Conservatives were level but the former could probably count on the votes of the minority parties. Armed with the promise of the king, the new Liberal government pushed through the Parliament Act, which meant that the Lords could only delay, not veto, legislation. The Lords caved in. The Liberals were now free to put their promised social reforms in the statute book.

DIFFERENCES WITHIN THE LABOUR PARTY

An important Royal Commission on the poor law had reported in 1909. In its minority report, George Lansbury sided with Beatrice Webb in arguing that insurance against sickness, unemployment, and old age should be the responsibility of the state. Far from that, when Lloyd George presented his National Insurance scheme in 1911, he proposed that contributions for sickness and unemployment benefits should be split between the employee (the largest amount), the employer, and the state. The Labour Party was at one in wanting an insurance act but divided over the form of insurance. Union-sponsored MPs tended to favour the government's proposal, particularly as Lloyd George had provided that much of it could be run through friendly societies linked with trade unions. Hardie, Snowden, and Lansbury argued fiercely that the scheme should be non-contributory, that is financed wholly by the state. In the vote, Hardie abstained while five Labour MPs voted against the government. All this angered MacDonald, who complained that Labour had for years done the groundwork yet the glory ended with the Liberals.

The internal Labour conflict continued. By this time, Hardie was less enthusiastic about the WSPU and acknowledged that the NUWS, which had grown rapidly in membership, had given up hope in the Liberals and was turning to Labour. Nonetheless, he continued to attack the government's approval of the ill-treatment, including forced feeding, of suffragettes in prison. George Lansbury stood with him and, enraged by the prime minister Asquith's offhand answers, rushed to the front and verbally abused him. He also regarded the Labour Party's tactics to further women's votes as ineffective and, in October 1912, he resigned his seat in order to re-contest it on the women's issue.

Hardie resigned from the Labour Party executive to campaign for Lansbury and they were joined by three other MPs, including Snowden. In the by-election the WSPU gave Lansbury little backing and he was defeated by the Conservative by 731 votes. MacDonald and other Labour MPs were furious with Lansbury and some of their anger was vented at Hardie.

Ironically, the anger of the WSPU was also directed at Hardie. Emmeline and Christabel Pankhurst condemned every MP who did not put the women's issue above all other parliamentary business. They even shouted him down at meetings. Dear old

Hardie was used to abuse and did not withdraw his support. In the Commons, he persuaded over fifty MPs to oppose the government's cat and mouse policy of preventing suffragettes from starving themselves in prison by releasing and then re-arresting them once they had recovered. Ironically, in June 1913, Hardie was invited by the pan-European Women's Suffrage Rally in Budapest as an honoured guest in recognition of his work for women. This was not the first time Hardie had been reviled at home and honoured abroad.

He also clashed with some colleagues over the start of a Labour daily paper. The *Labour Leader* was in decline, while several popular daily papers were anti-socialist. In March 1911 he made proposals to the ILP saying, "I want a daily paper that will be definitely socialist but which will give support to the Labour Party." He wanted it to come directly under the control of the more socialist ILP. His opponents added that it would also be more directly under his control. In the end it became a joint venture with the Labour Party and trade union money. Hardie withdrew. Launched in 1912, the *Daily Citizen* proved dull reading and collapsed within two years. Interestingly, the great Labour paper, the *Daily Herald*, was to develop from a strike sheet run by Lansbury and his colleagues.

During these years Hardie felt distant from some of his Labour MPs and worried that the Labour Party was becoming a party for Parliament, not for the people. For him, that was to change as Britain became engulfed in industrial strife so severe that Lloyd George later wrote that "by 1913 the country was on the verge of civil war".[11]

STRIKES

In many industries, wages had not risen in line with prices. A Board of Trade survey showed, for instance, that iron workers, some of the highest paid, received on average £82 a year while linen workers got £29. Yet prices were rising sharply and low pay did not seem to concern the affluent. Syndicalism, already known in Europe, found a hearing among left-wing workers. Its basis was that socialism could not be achieved by parliamentary methods and required continuous strikes by workers to bring down capitalism, with its replacement by the rule of workers. As mentioned, Tom Mann had returned from Australia and New Zealand, and he became the prophet of syndicalism. He urged workers to unite in larger organizations, for instance miners coming together in one union, in order to have a larger impact on employers.

A strike broke out in 1910 at the Cambrian Combine in Tonypandy, where its miners wanted parity with colliers working richer seams. Mann was soon there to encourage the strikers. So too was Hardie and he witnessed police brutality against miners and their families. Troops were also summoned by the Liberal government. In the Commons, Hardie denounced the brutality, to which the home secretary, Winston Churchill, asserted the need to defend the mine-owners' property. Hardie then cleverly linked the bringing in of troops as typical of the militarism of the so-called Liberal reformers.

This strike ended in failure but was followed by a seamen's strike, a national miners' strike, a dock strike, and more by other low-paid workers. Particularly significant was a national railway strike. It started in Liverpool, where porters wanted more than 17s. a week and escalated as the rail employers refused to recognize any of the four rail unions. Hardie immediately went to support the railway men in his constituency and spoke at a huge open-air meeting in Merthyr Park. He seized the opportunity to show the difference between Liberals and Labour, saying: "They will give you Insurance Bills, they will give you all kinds of soothing syrup to keep you quiet, but in the end your Liberal Party, just like your Tory Party, is the party of the rich, and exists to protect the rich when Labour and Capital come into conflict."

Looking around at the glorious scenery, he continued: "There is joy, beauty, peace, and prosperity everywhere, except in the homes and lives of the common people. Oh men and women, in the name of that God whom you profess to believe in, in the name of Jesus Christ of Nazareth who died to save your souls, how long do you intend to submit to a system which is defacing God's image upon you... which is blurring and marring God's handiwork, which is destroying the lives of men women and children?... fight for the coming day when in body, soul and spirit you will be free to live your own lives and give glory to your Creator." He sat down to "long and prolonged cheering".

A national strike did ensue and eventually recognition was given to the rail unions. The Liberal government then gave the impression that it had saved the day by skilful negotiation, a view accepted by the popular press. Hardie replied with a pamphlet of twenty-four pages, entitled *Killing No Murder! What Caused the Recent Railway Strike?*, to give the true story. He started by declaring that he regarded the strike "as the most momentous and significant event of modern times, and the action of the government as the most sinister and menacing of which this generation has had experience".[12]

He cited evidence to show that from the start the government had encouraged the employers not to make concessions and certainly not to recognize the unions. It assured them that troops would be used to protect the rail companies and to run some trains to ensure essential services. The prime minister, Asquith, was insistent that the troops would use force if necessary. When the employers declined to recognize the unions, a national strike was called. Hardie then made clear that the union leaders met with the Labour Party and with the Parliamentary Committee of the Trade Union Congress

(TUC). The meeting condemned the actions of the government and pledged support to the railway workers.

Soon 230,000 men were on strike. The government deployed 58,000 troops to guard stations and to ensure that some trains ran. In Llanelli two railway workers were shot and killed by soldiers and another two in Liverpool. Other unions declared their support and, with the prospect of the whole country grinding to a halt, the government pushed the railway companies into recognizing rail unions. MacDonald and Henderson were present at the meeting on 21 August when recognition was reluctantly given. Hardie emphasized that the strike had won the day, not a skilled government.

He then made some telling points in his pamphlet. One concerned the use of the army. Traditionally in Britain, the police kept law and order while the armed forces defended the country against foreign enemies. Now the Liberal government had placed the armed forces at the service of a private industry. The strike had shown the Liberal government in its true colours. "So long as it is a question of Insurance Bills that are being discussed the government is sweetness itself towards Labour and many are deceived. The moment Capital and Labour come into conflict... then the true affinity of the Liberal government is revealed."[13] The pamphlet ended: "There is but one solution for these recurring Labour troubles. The state must run the railways."[14] If nothing else, the railway strike had revealed the difference between the Liberal and the Labour parties.

Many more strikes followed and, indeed, continued to 1914. MacDonald thought they were dangerous. Henderson, great trade unionist though he was, was fearful of their growing militancy. It was Hardie who insisted on being in the thick of them. At the end of 1911 and the beginning of 1912 a coal strike was in the offing. In Wales, some pit-owners raised the price of coal and, in a bitter winter, the chief sufferers were the families of miners.

Hardie turned on the Cory Brothers, well known as church-goers and philanthropists, and wrote: "And the central fact is this: the respectable, church-going men who are, without cause, raising the price of coal in the depth of winter, and raising it most against the poor, are worse than common cheats and robbers. They are robbing the poor: not merely robbing them of money, but robbing them of comfort, of health, and, in some cases, of life… They may attend church or chapel regularly; they may give to charities and Christian missions; they may be respected members of society, patriots, and loyalists, but they are robbers all the same."

Later in 1912, he took up the case of the workers in the Dowlais Ironworkers in his constituency. Its owners, the strongly anti-union Guest, Keen, and Nettleford paid very low wages. In the Commons, Hardie pointed out that, as the men were working on a government contract, they were entitled to an agreed minimum wage. The government had to agree. The owners responded by a lock-out, which the men continued with a strike. King George V and Queen Mary were due to visit Merthyr in June 1912, so Hardie wrote (and published) a letter to them repeating the case and underlining that the workers had a twelve-hour day on a very low wage and lived in hovels from which the royal route was diverted. The owners backed down: the men were reinstated with their pay increase.

Hardie's participation in the industrial unrest of 1910–14 was important to both him and the Labour Party. Of course, he had always been involved in addressing public meetings, far more than any other Labour leader. But now it was akin to his early days as a trade union organizer as he met strikers face to face. There was a social excitement which, for Hardie, was a relief from the formality of Parliament.

Nonetheless, syndicalism was a problem for him. He applauded that it drew workers into action and organization. He acknowledged that its drive for an amalgamation of smaller unions into larger ones did make them more powerful. He added, in one speech, that this showed them to be "members of one class – fighting for the improvement of conditions all round". In short, this was working-class solidarity.

He was one of the few Labour heavyweights who saw anything positive in syndicalism and he declared in the Commons, "Syndicalism is the direct outcome of the apathy and indifference of this house towards working class questions and I rejoice in the growth of syndicalism." He was probably having a dig at colleagues who had become too attached to the Commons and too distant from working-class action. Notably, he did not say that he believed in syndicalism.

He was not a syndicalist. He was never in favour of violence ,whereas a section of that movement talked of strikes leading to the physical overthrow of Parliament. On the contrary, Hardie was a constant believer in democracy and in the expectation that eventually an elected Labour government would legislate for much public ownership. Indeed, this was why some syndicalists attacked him, arguing that working-class MPs, once in the Commons club, abandoned their socialism. By supporting strikes, by constantly being in the front line, Hardie's reputation as an extremist was magnified in the popular press. In fact, he was calling for organized and democratic protest but the Conservative and Liberal journalists gave him little credit for that.

Hardie became the link between strikers and the Labour Party. A number of Labour MPs, particularly Snowden, argued that the effectiveness of strikes was now over, that they were perceived by the public as dangerous, and that they achieved little. If made widespread, such a view would have alienated many strikers and other working-class activists from the Labour Party. By contrast, Hardie preached that strikes were the only way left for desperate workers, that they were the only response to hard-line employers, that many in the public were sympathetic to them, and that, in some cases, they did win substantial concessions. Hardie's sympathy for strikers, his presence among them, and his constant upholding of their case in print ensured that the link with the Labour Party survived.

It was Hardie, more than any other MP, who loudly proclaimed that the Liberal government called in soldiers to protect the owners of industry and even to shoot strikers. When the crunch came the Liberals put the interests of capitalists before those of Labour. He put the brake on any Labour merger with the Liberals. Morgan sums up the results of Hardie's actions at this time: "It enabled Labour to find a *via media* between the anarcho-syndicalists and the Lib–Labs. In so far as Hardie was a major architect of this achievement, it was one of his supreme contributions to the effective evolution of the British Labour movement."[15]

The industrial strife did not, as Snowden feared, lead to a backlash against Labour in local elections. Glasgow, by 1914, had eighteen ILP councillors. One was John Wheatley, who had formed the Catholic Socialist Society, which affiliated to the ILP. Wheatley played a big part in drawing Roman Catholics to the socialist cause, while later he became not only a Labour MP but a successful minister for housing.

Within the Commons, the Liberal government did introduce a Reform Bill in 1912 which extended the franchise – just for men. Under pressure from Labour, Asquith conceded that he would accept amendments to include women. Yet when Labour did just that in 1913, the Speaker ruled that they constituted a new bill. The government then withdrew its bill. The WSPU intensified its attacks on all parties. At least the year did see the Osborne judgment finally overthrown. Much credit went to MacDonald for his persistence both in keeping the matter on the political agenda and for persuading the Liberals to act.

Hardie continued to inspire and infuriate his parliamentary colleagues. Some did appreciate that he was a bridge between them and the Labour rank and file. Others resented his readiness to act without consulting them. In 1913 a large-scale transport strike started in Dublin under the charismatic if erratic James Larkin. Violence and deaths followed. Hardie hastened to the scene to express the support of the Labour movement, although the movement had not authorized him to do so.

Labour MPs may have been divided over Hardie. The popular press was almost wholly against him. But many working-class people greatly admired him. The ILP's annual conference in 1912 was held in Merthyr. It started with a powerful sermon from a local minister, the Revd Rowland Jones, who, like Hardie, preached that Christianity had to be expressed in the promotion of social justice. Hardie warned against the dangers of a return to being too close to the Liberals – probably another dig against MacDonald, who attended for only a short period.

FAMILY LIFE

At the Merthyr conference, Hardie introduced Lillie and Nan to Aggie, the daughter of the Hughes family, who, despite their own poverty, had so often provided hospitality for him. It was the start of a long friendship between Nan and Aggie.

In August 1912, the Hardies went on holiday to Arran, where one of Hardie's brothers lived. Hardie enjoyed it so much that he composed a Burnsian-style poem:

> A happy home, a loving wife
> An ILP fu' healthy
> I wadna' swap my lot in life
> Wi' any o' the wealthy.

Lillie also enjoyed the time in Arran but she might have wished for a larger slice from the wealthy.

It was a short holiday, for Hardie was off to the USA for two months. He was accompanied by a beautiful 33-year-old woman. Marian (usually known as May) Dalrymple Stoddart was the daughter of a Cumnock tailor. A trained nurse, she had long been in love with Jamie Hardie who, having put his earlier troubles behind him, had emigrated to the USA. Once he had established a carpet-cleaning business, he sent for May. They were married on 29 August 1912, with Hardie the only family member able to attend. Soon they bore the Hardies their first grandchild. Not surprisingly, Hardie found the time to address a few socialist meetings before returning.

In July 1913 Hardie boarded a train at Euston to attend an ILP summer school at Keswick. He collapsed and fortunately a colleague was able to put him in a taxi back to Neville's Court. Typically for Hardie, two days later he was at the conference and not only spoke but joined in the evening's singing and reels. Lillie was already there and afterwards they stayed on for a holiday.

Elizabeth Hughes, the mother of the Hughes family, died and Lillie and Nan invited Agnes to Lochnorris. They got on well together. Hardie praised his wife's wonderful cooking. Perhaps these three women shared their experiences as Labour supporters whose main task was to look after their men.

ILP CONFERENCE 1914

In 1914, Hardie again chaired the ILP and would be presiding at its twenty-first conference, to be held at Bradford, where it all started. Once there, he and other MPs were barracked by suffragettes but Hardie was not deterred. He was a founding father of the ILP and proud that it remained the most effective focus of socialism in Britain. After Henderson delivered a vote of thanks to him, he rose to lengthy cheering. He described the position in Britain twenty-one years before, saying: "it was tenaciously upheld by the public authorities, here and elsewhere, that it was an offence against the laws of nature and ruinous to the state for public authorities to provide for starving children and independent aid for the aged poor. Even safety regulations in mines and factories were taboo. They interfered with the 'freedom of the individual'. As for such proposals as an eight hour day, a minimum wage, the right to work, and municipal housing, any serious mention of such classed a man as a fool." He argued that Labour had promoted progress in all these areas and is "breaking down sex barriers and class barriers, is giving a lead to the great women's movement as well as to the great working-class movement".

He then changed tack in his speech, went back to his hardships in his early years as an MP and spoke emotionally about Lillie: "During those first three years my wife kept my house going, kept my children decently and respectably clothed and fed on an income which did not ever exceed 25 shillings a week." The audience interrupted to cheer Lillie and, in an unrehearsed addition, Hardie continued: "Comrades, you do well to honour her. Never, even in those days, did she offer one word of reproof. Many a bitter tear she shed, but one of the proud boasts of my life is to be able to say that if she suffered much in health and in spirit, never has she reproached me for what I have done for the cause I love."

In the Cumnock archives are copies of letters written by Hardie to Rose Davies, the young wife of a schoolmaster and keen ILP supporter in South Wales. Rose too was a trained teacher and socialist. Just before the 1914 conference, Hardie wrote to express disappointment that she could not attend: "I had been looking forward to seeing you and your sparkling eyes and cheeky smile. Yours sincerely, J. Keir Hardie." After the conference, he wrote again: "The conference was an inspiration. In all my experience I have never felt the same elation of spirit and that I suppose explains the high tone of my remarks to the children and again, at the close of the conference, especially the references to my wife." He continued about how much Lillie and Nan had enjoyed themselves.

The comment about the children referred to an address to them after they had sung to him at a nearby hall. He called on them to love flowers and animals, to fight poverty, and to work for peace. He finished, "If these were my last words, I would say to you, lads and lassies, live for the better day." The occasion was an example of how Hardie responded to children and how they responded to him. Years later, children remembered his exhortations. It moved Fenner Brockway, later the editor of the *Labour Leader*, to tears.

The happy reference to Lillie is also noteworthy: it is hardly the letter of a man who wanted a deep relationship with Rose, despite the affectionate tone of his earlier letter. He was encouraging her as a politician and, in the 1950s, she became the Labour chair of the Glamorgan County Council.

The penultimate words of his conference speech were to announce that he was standing down as chair so as not to stand in the way of younger members. He then closed with: "I shall die as I have lived, a member of the ILP... While I have anything to give, it shall be ungrudgingly to the child of my life – the ILP."

START OF THE FIRST WORLD WAR, 1914

Even as he spoke, world war was about to break out. Hardie had long foreseen a coming war and in his writings and in the Commons he often underlined the reasons why Britain would be drawn in. The government's imperial policy was to use the colonies as glorious trading centres, where British companies took local resources and bought and sold to their advantage. The companies looked upon British armed force to defend the colonies against the envy of other countries. He enumerated the constant growth in British army and naval power and predicted that this militarism would find its outlet in war. He detected that some private companies saw war as a means of making money, not only as they sold arms to the government but also horses, uniforms and vehicles. Not least, he deplored the Liberal government's secret diplomacy, which was committing Britain to action with other nations without the knowledge not only of the electorate but also of most MPs. The Socialist International of 1910 was held in Copenhagen. Hardie called for a general strike by all workers if war became imminent. Even his long-time colleague Bruce Glasier acknowledged that public opinion in every country would not respond to his call.

The assassination of Archduke Franz Ferdinand of Austria on 28 June led to Austria declaring war on Serbia. Germany backed Austria. Then Russia entered the fray. In the Commons, MacDonald argued eloquently that Britain had no reason to fight. Hardie wanted the country to be consulted. But on 4 August, following the German invasion of Belgium, Britain declared war.

To Hardie's dismay, public opinion, even that of the working class, was mainly for war. Most Labour MPs supported it and MacDonald, who held firm to his opposition, resigned the leadership of the party and was succeeded by Henderson. On 6 August Hardie was due to address a meeting in his constituency at Aberdare. He was jeered, shouted down, and his voice drowned under "Rule Britannia". As he left, he was hustled by a hostile crowd which, once he was in the home where he was staying, shouted, "Turn the German out."

It was the start of constant abuse in the streets, in railway carriages, and in the press. Emmeline Pankhurst had become a zealous supporter of the war and *The Suffragette* published a cartoon of the Kaiser giving money to Hardie with the lines, "Also the Nobel prize (though tardy), I now confer on Keir von Hardie." It even occurred in Cumnock, aimed not just at

Hardie but also his family. Lillie and Nan stood by him while Duncan opted to be a conscientious objector. He was pained when lifelong friends, such as George Barnes, backed the war. William Stewart stayed loyal and accompanied Hardie from Glasgow to Edinburgh to address a meeting. They were due to be met by a long-time supporter but instead received a message to say he had another engagement. William Stewart records that "Hardie understood… It was all part of the price."[16] Not least, in the battlefields over 2,500 soldiers were casualties every day, most of them working class, with a high proportion from Scotland. No wonder Hardie said, "I understand what Christ suffered in Gethsemane as well as any man living."

Devastated by the war and the insults, Hardie refused to retreat. In October 1914 he addressed another meeting in his constituency: this time in Merthyr, where he received a good reception. MacDonald accompanied him. Their opposition to the war had drawn them together again. In the Commons, Hardie pleaded for early peace negotiations and was called "coward". If a coward, he would not, despite failing health, have travelled all over the country arguing not only for peace but also for better material help for the families of soldiers sent abroad. In January 1915 he was one of the few journalists who reported the short Christmas truce between opposing troops on the western front. The pro-war lobby thought it was bad for morale.

At least the ILP stood firm, including a number of his old friends such as Bob Smillie. The ILP not only opposed the war, it also condemned the participation of any members in rallies to get men to join the army. It was the only party to stand apart and Hardie loved his child for its independence.

DEATH OF HARDIE

In January 1915 Hardie suffered a mild stroke. He refused to rest, although he was clearly ill. On 25 February he made his last major contribution in the Commons when he criticized the withdrawal of children from schools in rural areas to labour on farms. In what was perhaps his last article, he concluded with the hope that after the war, democracy would "break the rule of those to whom imperialism and militarism mean wealth and power, and install all the people of all lands in authority, and thus bring plenty, peace and concord to a long-suffering race". He went to a hydro in Caterham, Surrey. Lillie and Nan came to nurse him and they returned to Cumnock. He died of pneumonia in hospital on 26 September 1915. He was fifty-nine.

His funeral was held at Maryhill Crematorium in Glasgow, with his coffin followed by hundreds of working-class people. The Scottish custom that only men attended funerals was ignored. Lillie and Nan led the mourners, accompanied by Duncan and Hardie's brother George. Moreover, many women came to pay tribute to Hardie's stand for them. The Reverend A. M. Forson spoke about their work together in the Evangelical Union Church. Bruce Glasier, one of Hardie's great friends and critics, annoyed that no mention was made of his socialism, jumped to his feet and made an impromptu speech, saying that Hardie was the greatest agitator of his time. The next day, Nan wrote to a friend that what she missed most was the daily letter from her father.

Hardie left hardly anything save the house to his family, plus £96 still due from his parliamentary salary; so much for the myth about him making money. The ILP paid the funeral expenses and then put £500 in a trust, with the income paid to Lillie. This was later supplemented by a public appeal.

Honoured by family and the working class, not a word was said in tribute to him in the Commons. Noticeably, no representatives from other parties had been present at the funeral. Most newspapers had disliked him, as was reflected in those which did print an obituary.

The Times, always critical of Hardie, wrote: "It was Mr Hardie's misfortune that he inherited more than an average share of Scottish dourness. The spirit of compromise played but a minor part in his activities. This negatived much of his work for the party to which he belonged, while his imagination led him astray on many vital points. For example, his peculiar attitude on the war created a sharp cleavage between himself and his patriotic fellow Labourists."

The *Ayr Advertiser* gave much space to his first arrival at Westminster, saying that his "cloth cap, his rough tweed jacket, his flowing neck-tie, his unkempt hair and his obtrusive briar pipe were the evidence of a personal vanity". It added that in the last ten years in the Commons "he has been merely a unit, and by no means the most effective in the Labour Party, which he was mainly responsible for founding... As the parliamentary leader he was a failure... His early struggles to overcome poverty and ignorance left the mark in a narrow mindedness which he seemed to think an essential part of his creed."

The *Glasgow Herald* acknowledged that he was "a pioneer of socialist representation in parliament. But he was too advanced in his own views for the majority of his colleagues, and far too uncompromising in his advocacy of them, to be a successful parliamentarian, or to achieve any practical results."

At least the *Cumnock Chronicle* was more positive and paid tribute to his belief "in the independence of Labour in politics". It went on: "The women of the country had never a more vehement champion than Mr Hardie, for long before the question of 'votes for women' assumed the place in the political arena it came to occupy, he was trenchant and eloquent in his advocacy for simple justice being done to them." It summed up: "To our thinking, no single man has had a greater influence in forming the opinion – the political opinion – of the age in which we live."

Meetings were held in remembrance of Hardie. The ILP

organized a national memorial service in Glasgow, attended by 5,000, with many unable to get in. With Bob Smillie in the chair, the speakers included Ramsay MacDonald and Mary Macarthur. The latter thanked Hardie for fighting for both the political and industrial freedom of women.

The socialist press included many tributes to him. A piece by Bernard Shaw in the *Merthyr Pioneer* was entitled "Keir Hardie the Patriot". Deserted by Labour colleagues, lied to and abused by government ministers, Shaw wrote, "I really could not see what Hardie could do but die." He continued: "Everything that honest and humane men wish to defeat, discredit, and destroy in Germany, Hardie wished to defeat, discredit and destroy there; and he proved his sincerity by spending his life in trying to defeat, discredit and destroy here also… Let us hear no more about Hardie's lack of patriotism: he had more patriotism in his little finger than the government and its flatterers in all their bodies."[17]

Sylvia Pankhurst in 1932 published a moving account of the time she spent in the East End of London during the war. By that time, thanks to Hardie, she was as much a socialist as a suffragette. She occasionally saw Hardie and realized he was dying from the trauma of the war. She penned: "Dear Keir Hardie, how he was martyred by perpetual consciousness of that carnage. I had been awed by his misery at a mine explosion years before. Now in his deep eyes was the restless agony of a man in torment." Soon after this he died, and Sylvia added, "Keir Hardie has been the greatest human being of our time: when the dust raised by opposition to the pioneer has settled, this will be known by all."[18]

CHAPTER 9

THE MAN AND HIS LEGACY

This biography may be criticized as being too pro-Hardie. I have written it as a long-time admirer and one whose own beliefs and practices have been influenced by him. I do tend to be drawn to people who have come up the hard way and not on a path eased by affluent families and privileged education. Hardie was certainly one of these. No other Labour leader endured the poverty of his childhood and the harsh conditions of his mining jobs. George Lansbury also came through poverty in the East End of London but he never faced the dangers of work underground.

Of course, numbers of people do rise from humble beginnings. The government calls it social mobility and gives examples of individuals born to poor parents who become millionaires. What attracts me to Hardie is that he did not climb out of poverty to enrich himself but rather to improve the lives of others.

However, I will not ignore his failings. If any reader wants a strongly anti-Hardie chapter, I refer them to the attacks of Donald Carswell.[1]

It is difficult to separate Hardie from politics. However, in this chapter, I discuss him as a man, a politician, and a Christian. I then finish with a brief comment on his relevance today.

HARDIE THE MAN

He was often regarded as a grim, brusque figure. As cited in the last chapter, a national paper, in its obituary, dismissed him as having "more than an average share of Scottish dourness" With some reason: Hardie possessed a deep anger which probably stemmed from the cruel way he was treated by employers as a boy and a young man. He never lost his resentment at the offhand way in which politicians and owners of private companies dismissed the poverty, the ill health, the living conditions, and the deaths of working-class people. He could certainly be abrupt and dour with them. David Lowe, who was close to Hardie and his family, recorded: "He was a difficult man, reticent, stable in his mission, trusting few, friendly to the mass."[2]

The two sides of Hardie's character – the closed and the open – were well illustrated at a memorial service in Glasgow by Mary Macarthur. She told how she went to the Commons to see if Hardie would help a small body of struggling telephone girls. She said: "As he was speaking to me, one of the great and mighty ones came up and began to talk to Hardie praising something he had done. Hardie looked at him stiffly and coldly and said, 'I am engaged just now.'"[3] That very night he went to meet the telephone girls. Typically he was offended by the mighty and welcoming to the needy.

A number of observers noted how warm and affectionate he was with children. Fenner Brockway, for instance, recorded: "He made a practice of noting in his diary the birthdays of the children in the working-class homes in which he stayed during his visits about the country and, even when he was in the far parts of the world, never forgot to send them birthday cards."[4]

He would tell children stories about Roy the collie waiting for him in Cumnock or Donald the pit pony. For he also loved animals and would often stop in the street to pat a horse or stroke a stray dog. As Brockway continued: "He was the friend of the pit pony no less than the pitman, and raised his voice in parliament again and again to protest against the cruelties which mankind imposed upon their brothers of the field and forest."[5]

He was anything but dour at certain social occasions. At Independent Labour Party (ILP) and Scottish celebrations, he would join in the dancing and never required much persuasion to render, in his rich voice, "Mary of Argyle", "Robin Tamson's Smiddy", and other Scottish songs. By contrast, he was uncomfortable at and tried to avoid luxurious middle-class dinners and dances – unlike Ramsay MacDonald and Ethel Snowden, wife of Philip Snowden, who were increasingly attracted by fashionable company.

So Hardie was dour to some, delightful to others. Usually he favoured those from his own class background: but not always. He had several political working-class enemies, particularly among trade unionists who served as Lib–Lab MPs. Moreover, over time he could come to trust and like those of high rank. Cunninghame Graham is a good example.

Caroline Benn claims that Hardie "had few friends".[6] The evidence does not support this. Walter Forbes was a miner and union activist who always remained in touch with Hardie. He also met Bob Smillie in his mining days: they remained lifelong friends as Hardie went into politics while Smillie became a senior trade union official, and took the chair at the main memorial service in Glasgow after Hardie's death. In Cumnock, Hardie met William Small, a draper who studied mining legislation to identify the obligations of mine-owners toward their employees, and they saw each other when Hardie was home.

T. D. Benson was a long-serving treasurer of the ILP. He and Hardie respected each other and the respect grew into friendship. Benson was an affluent man and sometimes Hardie and Lillie would take a break at the Bensons' house.

Frank Smith, Bruce Glasier and his wife Katherine, and David Lowe were probably his closest friends. They stayed loyal to him from his earliest political days, in friendships that survived some differences of opinion. In the new year of 1897, Hardie wrote to Lowe: "Dear Dave, May the Lord be unto thee during the coming years what thou hast been unto me during the one now closing. I think there are cheerier days ahead." Their friendship tolerated arguments over political strategies, although Hardie could retreat in a huff. In May 1900 he wrote to apologize, stating: "Dear Dave, For the past ten days I have been in a sulking mood, and the garden has been the gainer." They were soon reconciled.

These friends were mainly active socialists who travelled to meetings all over the country. Hardie stayed in many working-class homes during his travels and also formed friendships with some of his hosts. Mention has already been made of the Hughes family. The Revd John Hughes was a Methodist in the Merthyr constituency. He suffered from pneumoconiosis from his time in the pits and, as he was badly paid as a minister, he and his wife Elizabeth struggled financially. He backed Hardie's socialism and was faced with criticisms from some of his congregation, but he never wavered. One of his daughters, Agnes, took to Hardie and became a socialist activist for the rest of her life. Their son Emrys was sixteen when he met Hardie and soon became a follower. Hardie and Lillie maintained close connections with the Hughes and when, during the war (after Hardie's death) Emrys became a conscientious objector and was treated cruelly by the authorities, Lillie and Nan constantly supported him. After the war, he was almost Lillie's adopted son. He married Nan and in 1946 was elected to the Commons.

What of Hardie's home life? Some writers criticize his long absences from his family, point out that he gave them little money to live on, and hint that there was much tension between them because Lillie resented being left with the children for long periods.

It is true that Hardie spent much time away from home. For some years he had a constituency in Wales, the Commons in England, and his home in Scotland, while he was in constant demand to speak at meetings. It is true that he always had a low income so that Lillie maintained children and home on 25s. a week. She must have got tired out looking after small children, she must have felt lonely because her husband was away so much. At times she was worn and ill. But her persistence, her loyalty and the fact that she never reproached her husband for his vocation were signs of a strong marriage, not a weak one.

Hardie valued his wife and wrote to her most days. As Glasier, so often Hardie's companion, put it, "he is very loyal to her and I believe very attached to her".[7] He was overjoyed every time an ILP meeting paid tribute to her.

Hardie loved being with his children. He recalled taking Nan and Duncan to the circus – by this time Jamie was working in Glasgow – even though he had to beg for free tickets. At times he thought longingly about life at Lochnorris. In a letter to David Lowe, written from home probably in 1901, he wrote:

The desire to make socialism understood is growing into a passion. I see no other chance for redeeming the world from poverty and uncleanness. But my solitary candle is burning low in its socket. Outside the twinkling stars are keeping watch over the silent world. What a blessed thing is the holy calm of this house retreat. Not a sound to be heard save the slow tick of the old grandfather clock on the stairs and the soothing murmur of the Lugar water at the foot of the garden. London is a place which I remember with a haunting horror, as if I had been confined there once in some long ago stage of a former existence… Here there are warm hearts and – peace. Where these are, heaven is.

Nothing better describes the commitment to socialism that so frequently took him from the family and place he loved best.

No one understood the relationship between the Hardies better than Nan, who lived at Lochnorris for much of her life. In 1939, as the provost of Cumnock, she unveiled a bronze bust of Hardie by Benno Schotz – it is still there in front of the town hall. In her acceptance talk, reported in the *Cumnock Chronicle,* Nan spoke movingly about her parents, saying:

> I know, perhaps only God and myself know just how much my mother did to help my father – the sacrifices which she made and the loneliness of her life. I am glad to know that my father has put it on record how much he owed to her. There are one or two little things which have hitherto been unknown. On his return from India, he wrote a book and had one volume specially bound for my mother. On this he wrote, "To Lily, without thee this book na'er had been". On the twenty-fifth anniversary of their wedding, he gave her money, and, as her wedding ring was wearing thin, he bought her a new one on which was inscribed, "To Lily, my leal-hearted wife and help-mate, with deathless love from Jamie."

Lillie was not an outgoing, playful woman. She was quiet, determined and loyal. Benn notes that Emrys Hughes stated that after Keir and Lillie settled in Cumnock "the bonds of sympathy and understanding between them grew".[8]

Most modern biographers of Hardie underestimate Lillie's support for his mission. They were not divided politically. Once the children were in their teens, Lillie frequently accompanied her husband to meetings and always to general elections. During the war, she steadfastly stood by his side, despite the jeers, and a few months before his death they stayed with Lillie's sister in Hamilton so they could attend an ILP meeting. After his death, she was disgusted that Cumnock council refused to erect a statue in his honour. She was gladdened when Nan took up with Emrys Hughes who, in his values and practices, was almost the successor to Hardie.

In 1924, the ILP held a conference in Cumnock during which Bob Smillie and James Maxton MP visited Lillie at Lochnorris with a token of their esteem. Benn records that Nan responded: "We have a Labour government but my father's work is not done. It will not be done so long as a child is born in hunger."[9] Lillie, although in poor health, reaffirmed her faith in the cause of her husband in her dignified way. Shortly afterwards she died.

Nan went on to become a Labour councillor in 1933 and then provost. Under her leadership, three-quarters of the town's population was rehoused in council dwellings, while a swimming pool and park were opened. This was municipal socialism that would have gladdened Hardie's heart.

It is a tribute to Hardie's character that his dedication to socialism did not alienate his immediate or extended family. Their son Duncan was a war resister but in 1921 he died after a tragic accident at work. Jamie had emigrated to the USA and Hardie had accompanied May Dalrymple Stoddart, a suffragette from Cumnock, there to marry him. It was May who maintained contact with the Hardies in Britain and they named their child Jean Stoddart Keir Hardie.

Two of Hardie's half-brothers followed him into the mines, socialism, and politics. In 1910 David was elected to the town council of Rutherglen, which then elected him as Labour MP in 1931. Unfortunately, he soon lost his seat following MacDonald's abandonment of Labour. George married Agnes Agnew Pettigrew, a well-known socialist who became women's organizer for the Labour Party in Scotland. In 1922,

George was elected MP for the Glasgow seat of Springburn and, on his death in 1937, he was succeeded by his wife.

None of Hardie's immediate or wider family ever wrote critically about his relationship with Lillie. They remained his supporters and admirers until their deaths.

POLITICAL CHARACTERISTICS

Turning to Hardie the politician, the danger is of portraying him as the sole creator of the Labour Party. This is far from the case. Senior figures who became MPs included Ramsay MacDonald, Arthur Henderson, and Philip Snowden. Smillie and Henderson, again, were prominent in trade union affairs. George Lansbury was another great socialist evangelist. Hard-working activists, some of whom recorded their involvement, were Frank Smith, Bruce and Katherine Glasier, David Lowe, William Stewart, Fenner Brockway, and Rose Davies, among others. Then there were thousands who joined the ILP, supported and campaigned for it, and in many cases were elected to local councils. The emerging Labour Party was a mass movement. Yet probably every member of the mass knew the name of Keir Hardie. He was their first MP, the first chair of the ILP, the first leader of the parliamentary party.

As a politician, contemporaries frequently pointed to three of his features or characteristics. His courage was evident in the way he stuck to his mission to go from being a penniless mining official to a not very well-off MP. Hardship and endurance were a part of his life he accepted. Glasier observed: "No man I have ever known had so deeply in him the capacity to stand alone, to fight alone, to win alone, and to be defeated alone."[10] In like manner, Emrys Hughes said: "To stand alone as Keir Hardie did in the House of Commons, scoffed at, shouted down, and to continue on undaunted and uncorrupted, demanded great strength of character and supreme courage. These were the qualities that marked Keir Hardie out from other politicians of his day."[11] Never was this better illustrated than in his dogged republicanism. He frequently attacked the royal family as undemocratic, extravagant, and uncaring about working-class people. Almost every MP, including those in his own party, failed to back him but he would not withdraw.

He was also incorruptible. He scorned the Liberals who promised him a safe seat and an annual salary if he stood down at one election. He declined numerous offers of money if he would promote a particular cause in Parliament. For a man in near poverty with a family to support, the offers must have been tempting but he never succumbed. Years later, Bob Smillie wrote that his home contained "a portrait of my dear old friend, Keir Hardie, one of the most unselfish souls who ever devoted life and talents to the class from which he sprang".[12] Of course, there were those who accused him of selfishly using politics to become an MP and leader. To be fair, however, Hardie was ever willing to give up these positions. Those who saw him frequently knew that he was devoted to others rather than self and this made him incorruptible.

Not least, he had the capacity to inspire others. Not just the great crowds but individuals to whom he gave time. He was almost a role model to Emrys Hughes. Fenner Brockway, in an interview placed with the Cumnock archive, tells how he went to interview Hardie for a newspaper. Brockway said: "He emphasised how his socialism was a human socialism, an ethical socialism. I think then he was an earnest Christian... he impressed me so much that I had gone to him a young Liberal, I left him a young socialist." Under Hardie he became a conscientious objector, editor of the *Labour Leader* and later an MP.

Hugh Dalton met Hardie when he came to speak at Cambridge University in 1907. Hardie was attacked by Tory students before he escaped. Dalton remembered: "In a crowded room I sat at his feet, literally and spiritually. I admired his total lack of fear or anger, his dignified bearing, his simplicity of speech and thought and faith. That night I became a quite convinced socialist."[13] Dalton, much later, became a Labour cabinet minister. Hughes, Brockway, and Dalton reflect many who met and were moved by Keir Hardie.

SOCIALIST EVANGELIST

Whatever his political features, I regard his greatest contribution to the Labour movement as that of socialist evangelist. He regarded his public speaking as his most important activity. As Bruce Glasier expounded: "For over 20 years he addressed meetings almost every night, often speaking twice on Saturdays and twice or three times on Sundays, travelling long distances, neglecting meals, conferring with local comrades far into the night."[14] He often tramped miles to speak, just as many tramped miles to hear him. Some meetings were indoors, some in the open air. Some attracted only a few listeners but as knowledge of him grew, so did the numbers, even reaching 300,000. Moreover, at the end of the talk, he did not slip away – as so many modern politicians do – but chatted with individuals as long as they wished before accompanying his hosts to their cottage. And he loved it. Commons committee meetings might have bored him, but never coming face to face with working-class crowds.

In 1908, Hardie said, "I am an agitator. My work has consisted of trying to stir up divine discontent with wrong." He wanted to inform his audience of their basic rights, of their rightful claim to work, a proper wage and decent housing. He added that only as they acted together could these ends be achieved.

His use of the word "divine" is appropriate, for his meetings were almost religious in character – in Wales the crowds did sometimes burst into hymns. Hardie was a preacher and he converted many people to socialism. For socialism was his theme: a moral belief that human suffering was wrong and that only by working-class action to secure the public ownership of industries and the redistribution of income and wealth could the good society be promoted.

Hardie was not a great theorist. But he succeeded in taking the message of socialism to hundreds of thousands of ordinary people in all parts of the British Isles. Many of his contemporaries were better writers, negotiators, and parliamentarians but none matched him in his outreach to the masses formerly excluded from politics. It could be said that he politicized thousands of working-class people.

As Benn put it so well: "He and his contemporaries, but especially Hardie, were able to change the way a whole generation thought about what was possible, putting before people an alternative social vision that gave their work tremendous power, a power that is all but lost to today's politics of the left."[15] And his efforts were successful, as more and more voted Labour. When he died in 1915, Hardie may have been in despair over the war. Yet eight years later, Labour won 191 seats and formed a minority government. That would not have seemed possible when he first stood for Parliament.

It is difficult to pin down what made Hardie such an effective speaker. He did not possess the fluency, the well-rounded sentences, the logic, the beautiful voice which made MacDonald a more acceptable performer in the Commons. He did not move around the platform, did not make dramatic gestures, apparently only rarely prepared his addresses. Hardie himself said he was not an orator.

Even his friends found it hard to explain why Hardie won such enthusiasm from working-class audiences. Stewart emphasized his clarity of expression, his ability to explain socialism in straightforward terms, and added that when "closing a speech on a note of passionate appeal the last word of the last sentence would ring out like the sound of a trumpet and call his auditors involuntarily to their feet; they knew not why except that they had to get up and cheer".[16]

Brockway, who often heard him speak, said the following in an interview: "He spoke so directly, so simply, so identifying himself from his own experiences from the wrongs which the working class were suffering so directing his appeal to them that they must form their own party and that they must have the aim of transforming society itself. His speech was so direct as though he was expressing his ingenuous inner self that it had tremendous effect on audiences."

Cunninghame Graham heard him at the hustings at West Ham when Hardie's Ayrshire accent went forth to cockney hearers. He observed that whereas most speakers patronizingly addressed the crowd as "gentlemen", Hardie always called them "men", so identifying himself with them. His heart went out to them and theirs to him and Cunninghame Graham concluded that he "has something poetic about his personality and his speech".[17]

The utter sincerity of the man came over in his talks. Unlike most political speakers, he was of their class, of their near poverty, who knew what it was like to be sacked. Yet, as one of them, he offered a different future and many responded.

His concentration on the working class was politically important. Early on he declared, "I am anxious and determined that the wants and wishes of the working classes shall be made known and attended to in parliament." Moreover, he believed that many working-class people had the talents to be MPs. After Snowden left the Labour Party and was elevated to the rank of viscount, he still expressed his admiration for Hardie, saying: "The moving impulse of Keir Hardie's work was a profound belief in the common people. He believed in their capacity and he burned with indignation at their sufferings."[18]

THE INDEPENDENT LABOUR PARTY

But the working class had no political party of their own. Once they got the vote, they had to use it for the aristocrats, lawyers, and commercial giants of the Liberal and Conservative parties. It follows that Hardie's next greatest achievement was the creation of the Independent Labour Party. Once again, this was not just him. Joseph Burgess, Ben Tillett, Pete Curran, and his usual colleagues were involved. Nonetheless, Hardie was at the centre and always regarded the ILP as his child. And it was a child that remained loyal, even once the First World War commenced. Fenner Brockway, reflecting years later in his interview on the contribution of Hardie, said that it "developed from a conviction that the working class had no hope in the upper middle class dominated Liberal Party. They must form their own party" – which came in the form of the ILP. It changed the nature of British politics.

Professor Morgan claims that the Labour electoral victory in 1945, when millions of working-class votes came its way, was Hardie's "supreme achievement".[19] This claim may be exaggerated, as the growth in the working-class vote also depended upon changes in attitudes wrought by the Second World War. What is more certain is that once New Labour abandoned Hardie's loyalty to the working class and his conception of socialism as essentially ethical, then any genuine commitment to equality and fraternity was undermined.

As far as Hardie was concerned, it was the *Independent* Labour Party. He fought many battles to ensure that it did not amalgamate with the Liberal Party. At times MacDonald, who was personally friendly with a number of Liberal MPs, wanted much closer ties. Some trade union MPs hankered after the position of the old Lib–Lab MPs who had accepted the Liberal whip in return for favours to trade unions and money for themselves. Another of Hardie's contributions was to maintain

Labour as separate. Even when the Liberal reformers presented themselves as more Labour than Labour, he consistently pointed out that it was still the party of capitalism which sent in the army to break up strikes.

His fear of and suspicion of the Liberals continued even when they came bringing gifts. His feelings may well have been expressed in his gruffness toward some Liberal MPs. His opponents claimed that his insistence on independence might have cost Labour certain concessions from the Liberals. In fact, the Liberals still passed the Trades Disputes Act, the reversal of the Osborne judgment and legislated salaries for MPs. He was accused of being too rigid and inflexible. He was even taunted with being a narrow Marxist.

Oddly enough, Hardie could also be very politically flexible. Within the ILP, he fought off the Social Democratic Federation (SDF) who wanted to restrict membership to socialists. In 1912, his friend and admirer Fred Jowett proposed it should concentrate much more on militant class issues but Hardie was among those who defeated him. He was also ready to receive middle-class people into membership provided they were ready to work with, not just for, the working class. He was wary of the ILP becoming pure in its socialism but lacking in support from many other Labourites.

Similarly, Hardie insisted that trade unions that joined the Labour Party did not have to commit themselves to socialism. Otherwise the party would have lost their votes. This did not mean he abandoned socialism. His talks and his writings – of which not enough has been written here – constantly proclaimed socialism. His argument was that once in the Labour Party, members might well be drawn to the socialist faith. But without a mass membership, political power could not be achieved.

Again, Hardie was prepared to accept and support some Liberal reforms. Indeed, he boasted that it was the Labour movement which first popularized welfare reforms. He saw them as steps, even though small steps, toward the socialist society. The ILP was independent but this did not rule out co-operation with other parties provided that political separation was maintained. Hardie's strategic genius was to obtain a balance between independence and flexibility. This ensured the continuation of the party and drew in a wide range of supporters without compromising on the existence of a working-class movement.

THE PARLIAMENTARIAN

"I wouldn't say he was a great parliamentary leader. He was too direct in his speech. He hadn't got parliamentary diplomacy." These words came not from an enemy of Hardie's but from one of his great followers, Fenner Brockway. He saw him as a great politician but better outside the Commons than inside. It was a view shared by many contemporaries and most modern writers. And it was admitted by Hardie himself. He had entered the Commons because he believed that working-class people should be there and the door opened while he was at West Ham. Yet he always longed to escape. He disliked the conventions, the archaic customs and language, and the scheming and dealing between members. Unlike MacDonald, he did not enjoy negotiating alliances, while committees often bored him.

He was said to lack "plasticity", that is a readiness to compromise with other parties and this, in turn, caused them to see him as self-righteous and not one of the Commons club. He was also unhappy as leader of the Parliamentary Labour Party (PLP) in 1906–7. He was not good at moulding his MPs into a team and he could lose patience with them. Significantly, after that year he never again held a position of authority or leadership in the parliamentary party.

That said, there is a danger of overlooking the positive factors about his performance in the Commons. His lack of plasticity enabled him to maintain the Labour Party as a separate and distinct group, even when it looked as though its few MPs would be swallowed by the Liberals. At times he did display the patience and capacity to amass detailed material to strengthen his speeches. No one in the Commons knew more about unemployment than he did; indeed the credit for keeping the topic on the parliamentary agenda goes largely to him.

Further, he was prepared for the hard grind of getting through what seemed to be insignificant legislation. For instance, Aggie Hughes, sister of Emrys, campaigned for safer railways and two more stations to suit the needs of miners in Abercynon. To obtain this, Hardie had to block a private railway bill before these apparently small improvements could benefit the miners. In the same manner, he asked numerous questions about the plight of paupers, the cruel treatment of suffragettes, and the violence towards strikers by the police.

At times, when Hardie rose to speak, members groaned. But frequently his dogged attacks on the administration of the poor law, his revelations of the sufferings of the poor in comparison with the luxuries of the royal family, and his persistent warnings that militarism would lead to war won attention and respect. He was not as good at engaging in the cut and thrust of debate but everyone in the Commons knew what he stood for.

Before leaving Parliament, it is worth mentioning two areas where Hardie had a long-term effect. One was welfare legislation. When Hardie was young, there was virtually no welfare legislation save for the punitive poor law. There were charities and Hardie was close to the Salvation Army but he pointed out that charities came and went, were strong in some places and weak in others, and often had their conditions set by the rich. He countered that just welfare had to be state welfare and, in the Commons, he frequently made the case for unemployment pay, old-age pensions, health care, and council housing, all paid for by taxes.

Under Gladstone, the Liberals were opposed to state intervention in welfare – as were the Conservatives. Hardie and his colleagues stood for the opposite and clearly attracted working-class votes. In 1906, the Liberal Party took welfare on board. Today's welfare state is often traced back to the Liberal reformers. The tracing should be extended to Hardie and his colleagues, who planted the welfare seeds which were reaped by the Liberals.

Up to the time of Hardie, imperial or colonial policy in Parliament took it for granted that colonies in Asia, Africa, and elsewhere were outlets for trade, sources of resources and cheap labour, and should be permanently under white rule. Hardie's visits to South Africa and India, followed by his then frequent correspondence with indigenous residents, led to his famous critique of Britain's racist rule and his pleas for much more involvement of black and brown people in government and administration. His proposals met furious opposition within the Commons for, as Iain McLean explained: "The idea that India might eventually become a self-governing dominion was revolutionary in 1907."[20]

A few Liberals were impressed by Hardie's courage and values. But his greater influence was within his own party. Few Labour MPs, except MacDonald, had taken much interest in the colonies. To cite McLean again, "Hardie was the first Labour politician to express concern at the status of non-white citizens of the British empire."[21] Gradually Labour MPs did voice colonial policies in Parliament, which culminated in the granting of independence to India, Ceylon, and Burma under the Attlee government. Not long after, even Conservatives accepted the need for change.

HIS CHRISTIANITY

It is not known just when Hardie gave up his membership of the Cumnock Evangelical Union church. Probably in the early 1890s, when he spent much more time in London and then moved there when he was elected at West Ham.>

Some writers say little about his Christianity after his activities in the Evangelical Union church and assume that his religion became much less important to him. My reading is that Christianity continued as a main factor – and probably the main factor – which drove his life. There is no evidence that, thereafter, Hardie became a regular worshipper at a particular church – which would have been difficult given his frequent travelling and numerous speaking engagements. Almost nothing is known about his attention to prayer and Bible-reading. Nothing is recorded about Lillie's participation in church life. It is not even known whether they sent the children to Sunday school, although Hardie did have an interest in socialist Sunday schools.

What is sure is that he always regarded himself as a Christian. It rings out from scores of his articles and speeches. This was an age of many attacks on Christianity following the discoveries of Darwin, which appeared to undermine the biblical account of creation, and then books by liberal theologians that cast doubts on the divinity of Jesus. Benn states that Hardie's religion was identified with this liberal theology and "was not divinely based on God but on a human Christ".[22] She also asserts that, as he grew older, he was drawn into other religions, especially Buddhism and Islam.

Yet his statements showed that his Christianity remained rooted in traditional beliefs. He often cited verses from the Bible and accepted them as truth. As late as 1912, in a talk entitled "What think ye of Christ?" and delivered to strikers and their families, he demanded: "Oh, men and women, in the name of the God whom ye profess to believe in, in the name of Jesus of Nazareth who died to save your souls, how long do you intend to submit to a system which is defacing God's image upon you?"

His Christian belief still held to the veracity of Scripture, to God the creator, and to a divine Jesus who died to save people's souls. Conservative evangelicals, not liberal theologians, would have applauded.

He also believed in a Christ who lived alongside the poor, who warned about the evils of riches, and who taught the second commandment to love our neighbours. He believed that all people were equal before God. Addressing miners in 1885, he told them: "You are God's children. Your work is mining, but the blackest work to which a man may put his hand can never disguise or blot out the image of him in whose likeness he was made." Hardie's interpretation was that as all were made in the image of God then all should benefit from God's bounty. Riches, wealth, money, property should be shared. Many conservative evangelicals parted company with Hardie's social gospel but he insisted that it rested on God's revelation just as much as his teaching on more spiritual matters. In his book *From Serfdom to Socialism*, he had a chapter entitled "Socialism and Christianity" in which he expanded this point and illustrated it from both the Old and New Testaments.

And he stayed with these beliefs all his life. Certainly, he developed a great interest in eastern religions. So did F. B. Meyer, already mentioned as one of Britain's foremost evangelical ministers, whose life overlapped with that of Hardie. His contacts with Gandhi and other religious leaders in the east left him "impressed by their deep religiousness, charity, purity and self denial".[23] But Meyer still retained his Christian convictions. Coming up to date, a number of Christians work with destitute asylum-seekers. The latter often have strong but different faiths. The British participants come to respect their religions without abandoning their own. The same was true of Keir Hardie.

Christianity, not Marxism, was the basis of Hardie's socialism. In particular, within it he identified a morality which justified socialism. Inequality, poverty, class differences, and social distress were just wrong, for they undermined God's intention for the people of the world. It followed that their abolition and replacement by brotherhood and justice were values to be held by all Christians. As Gordon Brown put it, "His socialism in practice owed more to religion than to economics. Almost every speech or article of Hardie's endorsed this view."[24] Fenner Brockway, who was not a Christian, wrote: "His religious idealism determined the tone of his expression of socialism. 'Socialism', he said repeatedly, 'is a great moral movement. I am a socialist because socialism means fraternity based on justice.'"[25] Hardie proclaimed that socialism was "a question of ethics or morals… a handmaiden of religion and as such entitled to the support of all who pray for the coming of Christ's kingdom on earth". Nothing shows more explicitly that his socialism was rooted in Christianity.

But how was this morality to be achieved? Hardie claimed in 1912 that, for the first 300 years, Christians did not simply profess a belief in Christ; "they got to practising the doctrines of Christ by holding all things in common. There was no such thing known to the early Christians as private property." Subsequent Christians then shaped a different Christ, who encouraged the accumulation of wealth and property. It followed that the social practice of Christianity had to be pursued in an outside, secular body which held the same morals as the original Christians. That body was the socialist movement and it was not restricted to Christians.

Hardie never claimed that socialism replaced Christianity or the church. Indeed he insisted that people still needed God in a relationship sense. As he put it, "Life without religion would be so distasteful that did not religion exist, men would have to invent a religion to satisfy that part of their nature."

Nonetheless, Hardie did bring Christianity and socialism together in what was called Christian socialism. Of course, Hardie was not the first to recognize the social implications of Christ's teachings. Dr David Smith has detailed the rise and fall of the social gospel in Christendom, particularly in evangelical churches. He observed that William Wilberforce promoted the end of the slave trade – and relief for the poor – "while justifying the continuance of a hierarchical social system".[26] One result of such teaching was the continued separation of rich and poor Christians.

Some Christians did criticize the class-ridden works of people such as Wilberforce. They were usually middle-class Christians like F. D. Maurice and Charles Kingsley, who called themselves Christian socialists but who had little in common with the Christian poor. The Guild of St Matthew and the Church Socialist League made radical attacks on the government and on the churches but had few working-class followers. Hardie's great contribution was to bring Christianity and socialism together in his talks and articles. Speaking to vast working-class audiences, he frequently drew cheers and applause when he expounded the social nature of the gospel. He then encouraged his listeners to express these Christian principles in politics via the Labour Party.

Hardie once wrote, "Many have left the church in order to become Christians." Probably he included himself. In 1912 he was reported as saying: "Much has been said in these days about the failure of the working class to attend the church, but there was no mystery about that. The working class was not interested to know what Christ thought about the scribes and Pharisees 1,900 years ago: men and women now wanted to know what Christ thought about the scribes and Pharisees at the beginning of the twentieth century." He seethed at churches which reflected class differences; which defended wealthy members who allowed fellow Christians to live in hovels and die in poverty. He condemned respectable ministers who welcomed only respectable worshippers. Hardie was not respectable. He was illegitimate, his family had been desperately poor, he had been sacked and then banned as a strike leader, he was a republican and an opponent of war. Such an individual was not very welcome in establishment churches.

His deep anger against hypocritical Christians was most famously expressed in his campaign against Lord Overtoun. It was followed by others. Many church leaders rose up against him for attacking well-known Christians. Yet one positive outcome was that his campaigns resulted in better conditions and wages for the workers.

Too negative toward Christianity?

Was Hardie too negative toward the church and certain Christians? He could have devoted more space to Christian employers who did treat their staff well. During the Boer War, he railed against the clergy who supported it. But he said little about the minority who did oppose it. It must be remembered that Hardie himself had suffered at the hands of a wealthy Christian baker while his mother was pregnant and penniless. He often returned to this experience, which had left a deep resentment within his soul.

It is overlooked that Hardie did have positive relationships with a number of clergymen. As mentioned in Chapter 7, during the 1890s a number of nonconformist ministers, liberal and evangelical, drew together in what was called "the New Theology". They did not reject the spiritual gospel but acknowledged that the social gospel was also a true part of Christianity. Some began to rebel against the dominance of wealthy factory- and shop-owners in their congregations.

Some, especially in Merthyr, gave open support to Hardie in his campaigns against poverty, unemployment and inequality. A number provoked the hostility of their members. In 1910, when the evangelical Revd John Hughes was under attack from some of his congregation, Hardie went out of his way to write to express his support and thanks.

Hardie shared platforms with these ministers, sometimes preached in their churches, wrote in their journals. When he was elected first leader of the Labour Party, Hardie received 165 letters of congratulations from ministers. He was not separate from the church.

Regrettably Hardie did not, apparently, identify with one church after he left the Evangelical Union. It might have provided Christian fellowship outside politics and strengthened his spirituality by regular worship. But he certainly did try to live the Christian life. His teetotalism never faltered, he never displayed personal greed, and had a reputation for honesty and keeping his word. At his main memorial service, Bob Smillie said, "He was one of the most unselfish souls that ever lived. I never heard him speak of self… I never heard him express any great desire to accumulate wealth."[27] These characteristics are the imprint of Christianity.

There is something even deeper. I look at Hardie – yes, the sometimes gruff Hardie, in untidy clothes with a briar pipe usually hanging from his lips – and see Jesus not in his obvious goodness but in his lifestyle and sufferings. Like Jesus, he wanted to be close to working-class people. Like Jesus, he was not out to impress important politicians, royalty, religious leaders, and members of commercial and military elites. This cannot be said of many prominent Christians today.

Then he accepted personal abuse. The personal attacks and lies about him never ceased. Early in his parliamentary life, he printed the menus from which MPs gorged themselves and contrasted them with the lack of choice of the starving. They retaliated in the press with rumours that he was a glutton, smoked cigars costing 2s. 6d. each, and lived in a hotel where he enjoyed champagne and ten-course meals. He received hundreds of crude letters. At elections he was accused of advocating free love and being an atheist. Often when he rose in the Commons to make a case for the socially deprived he would be jeered, howled at, and interrupted.

When asked by his friends to hit back, he replied, "Let conduct be its own reward." Yet the continual misrepresentations, false accusations, and cruel cartoons must have been among the factors which sometimes depressed him and increasingly affected his health.

During the Boer War, he was declared to be anti-British and his meetings were raided by gangs. It was even worse in the First World War. At his memorial service, MacDonald said: "Because he had taken the stand he had, every miserable scoundrel in the country, backed up by disreputable papers, called him a traitor."[28] He was physically attacked, called a German, and almost hated by some MPs. He said, "I knew what Gethsemane was like." And he knew that after Gethsemane came death. He identified with Christ's sufferings and with his death.

Brockway recorded: "Towards the end of his life he said that were he to live it again he would devote it to the advocacy of the gospel of Christ."[29] This was not a statement of despair. He always recognized that Christianity was about hope and resurrection. When he died, thousands were being slaughtered every day and the Labour movement was split in twain. Yet Hardie foresaw better days. He was a remarkable politician and mainly so because he was rooted in Christianity. We should give thanks for him.

CHAPTER 10

Epilogue

I cannot pretend to write objectively about Hardie. Like him, I care passionately about Christianity and the Labour Party. I end this book by considering implications for the way in which Christians, Labour supporters and others may live today.

The churches

I believe that the attitude and teaching of the church – or the churches – toward money and wealth are not consistent with the life and teachings of Jesus. I have reread the gospel of Luke and have noticed how frequently Jesus warned about the dangers of riches and how he instructed his followers not to amass possessions and wealth. Yet the church rarely if ever admonishes affluent members who enjoy luxuries while others, even in Britain, are in dire poverty. I know no Christian leaders who name and shame greedy Christians in the way that Hardie did. The social and geographical gap between rich and poor Christians is as wide now as in his day. I believe with Hardie that the church and its members should identify with and be alongside those at the bottom of the social scale.

THE LABOUR PARTY

Further, I believe that politicians should heed Hardie's warnings about "the dangers" of the Commons. He saw working-class MPs lose their convictions because of "the unlimited opportunities for meeting wealthy people and being patronised by society". Certainly I have known young MPs whose loyalty to their original principles has been eroded by being members of the Commons, "the best gentlemen's club in Europe". They become less comfortable in the company of needy people and soon live well distant from them. Even when leader of the party, Hardie spent as much, if not more, time with working-class supporters as with MPs.

As an MP, Hardie often survived in near poverty. Yet he did not support the proposal to pay MPs £400 a year. He argued that it would draw in those who saw politics as a means to a money-making career. He was right, as is demonstrated by the number of MPs who supplement their very high salaries with consultancies and directorships. My belief is that MPs should accept only a modest amount so that they never lose physical and social touch with those whose lives the Labour Party was created to transform. Hardie never ditched his commitment to, understanding of, friendships with, and empathy for working-class people.

THE ENVIRONMENT

The implications of Hardie's lifestyle are not just for Christians and Labour supporters. Almost before his time, he had a concern for the environment. His contact with Lord Overtoun's chemical works showed how fumes poisoned the air in which men toiled, while poisoned waste was poured into the river. He discovered that such practices were commonplace. He urged local authorities to take action and, nine years later, he was calling for the central government to prevent coastal erosion and to renew forests which were being commercially exploited.

Today concerns for the dangers to the environment of climate change are more widespread. Some realize that the huge demands for fuel, heat, wood, and other basic resources are reaching the point where they could soon be exhausted. What can be learned from Hardie? He and his family lived very modestly, sometimes because they lacked the money but also when they had sufficient. A reporter noticed that they had few luxuries in their home. He grew the family's own vegetables and fruit. He ate sparingly and healthily. He declined invitations to freebie public dinners. He never travelled above third class and, if not getting hospitality with a family, lodged in a cheap temperance hotel. He spent little on clothes – sometimes to the sneers of other MPs. His demands on resources were small.

Today a number of other people are also living modestly. If on a high salary, they take sufficient for their family's needs and give the surplus to good causes. They may live in cheap houses in non-fashionable neighbourhoods. They rarely holiday abroad, limit expenditure on food, electrical goods and petrol. As a sizeable proportion of CO_2 emissions come from private households, they are cutting theirs and so playing a part in reducing adverse climate change. Simultaneously, they limit the demands they make on vital resources. People following this pattern may be of any faith or no faith. The example of Hardie can be an inspiration for all people worried about the future of the world.

SOURCES AND
BIBLIOGRAPHY

The Baird Institute in Cumnock contains the Hardie Room and a mass of Hardie material: not only books and pamphlets by and about him but also photographs, original documents and letters, newspapers, and also copies of documents which are located in other places. Unfortunately, this material is not well indexed, indeed some is just put into files or boxes.

The newspapers and journals from which I have quoted are as follows: *Ardrossan and Saltcoats Herald, Ayr Advertiser, Christian Commonwealth, Cumnock Chronicle, Daily Mirror, Daily News and Leader, Daily Record and Mail, Glasgow Herald, Kilmarnock Herald, Kilmarnock Standard, Labour Leader, Merthyr Pioneer, The Miner, The Thinker, The Times, Workman's Times, West Ham Herald.*

Particular mention must be made of the book edited by Emrys Hughes, *Keir Hardie's Speeches and Writings 1888–1915* (Glasgow: Forward Printing and Publishing Company, 1927), which contains not only many of Hardie's talks and articles but also a biographical note by Hardie's daughter and Hughes's wife, Nan Hardie Hughes, and a reprinted article by George Bernard Shaw entitled "Keir Hardie the Patriot".

The main books and pamphlets which I consulted were as follows:

Benn, Caroline, *Keir Hardie*, London: Richard Cohen Books, 1997. First published 1992.

Booth, Charles, *Life and Labour of the People*, vol. 1, London: Williams & Norgate, 1889.

Booth, William, *In Darkest England and the Way Out*, London: Salvation Army, 1890.

Braisford, Henry Noel (pamphlet), *The Memory of Hardie*, London: ILP, undated.

Brown, Gordon, *Maxton*, Edinburgh: Mainstream Publishing, 1986.

Carswell, Donald, *Brother Scots*, London: Constable & Co., 1927.

Cole, Margaret, *Makers of the Labour Movement*, London: Longmans, Green & Co., 1948.

Cole, Margaret, *The Story of Fabian Socialism*, London: Heinemann, 1961.

Dale, Graham, *God's Politicians. The Christian Contribution to 100 Years of Labour*, London: HarperCollins, 2000.

Davis, Mary, *Sylvia Pankhurst. A Life in Radical Politics*, London: Pluto Press, 1999.

Foote, Geoffrey (ed.), *The Labour Party's Political Thought. A History*, Beckenham: Croom Helm, 1986.

Fraser, Hamish and R. Morris, (eds), *People and Society in Scotland 1830–1914*, Edinburgh: John Donald, 1990.

Fyfe, Hamilton, *Keir Hardie*, London: Duckworth, 1935.

Glasier, J. Bruce (pamphlet), *Keir Hardie. The Man and His Message*, London: ILP, 1919.

Guardian (pamphlet), *First World War. The Road to War*, London: The Guardian, 2008.

Hamilton, Mary, *Arthur Henderson. A Biography*, London: Heinemann, 1938.

Haw, George, *From Workhouse to Westminster. The Life Story of Will Crooks*, London: Cassell, 1907.

Hardie, J. Keir (pamphlet), *Can a Man be a Christian on a Pound a Week?*, London: ILP, 1901.

— — (pamphlet), *John Bull and the Unemployed*, London: ILP, 1905.

— — (pamphlet), *The Citizenship of Women. A Plea for Women's Suffrage*, London: ILP, 1906.

— —, *From Serfdom to Socialism*, London: George Allen, 1907

— —, *India. Impressions and Suggestions*, London: ILP, 1909.

— — (pamphlet), *Killing No Murder! What Caused the Recent Railway Strike?*, London: ILP, 1911.

Heasman, Kathleen, *Evangelicals in Action*, London: Geoffrey Bles, 1962.

Holman, Bob, *Trading in Children. A Study of Private Fostering*, London: Routledge, Kegan & Paul, 1973.

— —, *Good Old George. The Life of George Lansbury*, Oxford: Lion Publishing, 1990.

— —, *F. B. Meyer. "If I Had a Hundred Lives..."*, Fearn: Christian Focus Publications, 2007.

Hughes, Emrys (ed.), *Keir Hardie's Speeches and Writings 1888–1915*, Glasgow: Forward Printing and Publishing Co., 1927.

Hughes, Emrys, *Keir Hardie*, London: Allen & Unwin, 1956.

Johnson, J. Francis (pamphlet), *Keir Hardie's Socialism*, London: ILP, 1922.

Lean, Garth, *Brave Men Choose*, London: Blandford Press, 1961.

Lowe, David, *From Pit to Parliament. The Story of the Early Life of James Keir Hardie*, London: Labour Publishing Co., 1923.

Mackenzie, R. T., *British Political Parties*, London: Heinemann, 1955.

McLean, Iain, *Keir Hardie*, London: Allen Lane, 1975.

Martin, Hugh (ed.), *Christian Social Reformers in the Nineteenth Century*, London: SCM Press, 2nd edition, 1933.

Maxton, James, *Keir Hardie. Prophet and Pioneer*, London: Francis Johnson, 1939.

Mayor, Stephen, *The Churches and the Labour Movement*, London: Independent Press, 1967.

Morgan, Kenneth, *Keir Hardie. Radical and Socialist*, London: Weidenfeld & Nicolson, 1984. First published 1975.

Pankhurst, Sylvia, *The Home Front*, London: The Cresset Library, republished 1987.

Pelling, Henry, *The Origins of the Labour Party 1880–1900*, London: Oxford University Press, 1976. First published 1965.

Reid, Fred, *Keir Hardie. The Making of a Socialist*, London: Croom Helm, 1978.

Reid, Fred, "Hardie's Laurels", *Tribune*, 3 July 1992.

Romero, Patricia, *Sylvia Pankhurst. Portrait of a Radical*, New Haven: Yale University Press, 1987.

Rowntree, B. S., *Poverty. A Study of Town Life*, London: Macmillan, 1901.

Smillie, Robert and others, *Memoir of James Keir Hardie*, London: ILP, 1915.

Smillie, Robert, *My Life for Labour*, London: Mills & Boon, 1924.

Smith, David, "Evangelicals and Society", manuscript chapter, Glasgow, 2007.

Smout, T. C., *A Century of the Scottish People 1830–1950*, London: Collins, 1986.

Snowden, Ethel, *The Woman Socialist*, London: ILP, 1907.

Stewart, William, *J. Keir Hardie*, London: George Allen, 1921.

References

Introduction

1. David Lowe, From Pit to Parliament. The Story of the Early Life of James Keir Hardie, London: Labour Publishing Co., 1923, p. i.
2. Caroline Benn, Keir Hardie, London: Richard Cohen Books, 1997, p. xi.
3. Benn, Keir Hardie, p. xii.
4. Fred Reid, "Hardie's Laurels", Tribune, 3 July 1992, p. 5.
5. Kenneth Morgan, Keir Hardie. Radical and Socialist, London: Weidenfeld & Nicolson, 1984, p. vii.

Chapter 1

1. T. C. Smout, A Century of the Scottish People 1830–1950, London: Collins, 1986, p. 2.
2. Smout, Century of the Scottish People, p. 103.
3. Hamilton Fyfe, Keir Hardie, London: Duckworth, 1935, p. 61.
4. William Stewart, J. Keir Hardie, London: George Allen, 1921, p. 7.
5. Emrys Hughes (ed.), Keir Hardie's Speeches and Writings 1888–1915, Glasgow: Forward Printing and Publishing Co., 1927, p. ix.
6. Lowe, From Pit to Parliament, p. 81.
7. Donald Carswell, Brother Scots, London: Constable & Co., 1927, p. 164.
8. Fred Reid, Keir Hardie. The Making of a Socialist, London: Croom Helm, 1978, p. 38.
9. Graham Dale, God's Politicians. The Christian Contribution to 100 Years of Labour, London: HarperCollins, 2000, p. 21.
10. Iain McLean, Keir Hardie, London: Allen Lane, 1975, p. 4.
11. Benn, Keir Hardie, p.17.

CHAPTER 2

1. Carswell, *Brother Scots*, pp. 164–67.

2. Robert Smillie, *My Life for Labour*, London: Mills & Boon, 1924, p. 33.

3. Reid, *Keir Hardie,* p. 68.

4. Margaret Cole, *Makers of the Labour Movement*, London: Longmans, Green & Co., 1948, p. 225.

5. Smout, *A Century,* p. 190.

6. Lowe, *From Pit to Parliament,* p. 19.

7. Morgan, *Keir Hardie,* p. 9.

8. Emrys Hughes, *Keir Hardie*, London: Allen & Unwin, 1956, pp. 28–29.

9. Garth Lean, *Brave Men Choose*, London: Blandford Press, 1961, p. 167.

10. Benn, *Keir Hardie,* p. 38.

11. Geoffrey Foote (ed.), *The Labour Party's Political Thought. A History*, Beckenham: Croom Helm, 1986, p. 19.

12. Reid, *Keir Hardie,* p. 81.

13. Bob Holman, *Good Old George. The Life of George Lansbury*, Oxford: Lion Publishing, 1990, p. 26

14. Bob Holman, *F. B. Meyer. "If I Had a Hundred Lives..."*, Fearn: Christian Focus Publications, 2007, p. 97.

CHAPTER 3

1. Henry Pelling, *The Origins of the Labour Party 1880–1900*, London: Oxford University Press, 1976, p. 1.

2. Pelling, *Origins of the Labour Party,* pp. 6, 3.

3. J. Bruce Glasier, *Keir Hardie. The Man and His Message*, London: ILP, 1919, p. 6.

4. Morgan, *Keir Hardie,* p. 20.

5. James Maxton, *Keir Hardie. Prophet and Pioneer*, London: Francis Johnson, 1939, pp. 8–9.

6. Hughes, *Keir Hardie,* p. 39.

7. Benn, *Keir Hardie,* p. 54.

8. Pelling, *Origins of the Labour Party,* p. 64.

9. Pelling, *Origins of the Labour Party,* p. 65.

10. Benn, *Keir Hardie,* p. 59.

11. Benn, *Keir Hardie,* p. 46.

12. Maxton, *Keir Hardie*, p. 9.
13. Morgan, *Keir Hardie*, p. 32.
14. Reid, *Keir Hardie*, p. 103.
15. Lowe, *From Pit to Parliament*, p. 116.
16. Morgan, *Keir Hardie*, p. 22.
17. Benn, *Keir Hardie*, p. 60.

CHAPTER 4

1. Morgan, *Keir Hardie*, p. 45.
2. Reid, *Keir Hardie*, p. 136.
3. Benn, *Keir Hardie*, p. 79.
4. Lowe, *From Pit to Parliament*, p. 85.
5. Morgan, *Keir Hardie*, p. 67.
6. Pelling, *Origins of the Labour Party*, p. 116.
7. Hughes (ed.), *Keir Hardie's Speeches and Writings*, p. 30.
8. Morgan, *Keir Hardie*, p. 64.
9. Pelling, *Origins of the Labour Party*, p. 118.
10. Morgan, *Keir Hardie*, p. 64.
11. McLean, *Keir Hardie*, p. 51.
12. Glasier, *Keir Hardie*, p. 10.
13. Stewart, J. *Keir Hardie*, p. 94.
14. Benn, *Keir Hardie*, p. 123.
15. Holman, *F. B. Meyer*, p. 88.
16. McLean, *Keir Hardie*, p. 59.
17. Kathleen Heasman, *Evangelicals in Action*, London: Geoffrey Bles, 1962, p. 293.
18. Stephen Mayor, *The Churches and the Labour Movement*, London: Independent Press, 1967, p. 387.
19. Stewart, J. *Keir Hardie*, pp. 102–103.
20. The Webb and Burns comments are cited by Pelling, *Origins of the Labour Party*, p. 167.

CHAPTER 5

1. Benn, *Keir Hardie*, p. 127.
2. Ethel Snowden, *The Woman Socialist*, London: ILP, 1907, p. xxii.
3. Carswell, *Brother Scots*, p. 192.
4. Carswell, *Brother Scots*, p. 207.
5. Carswell, *Brother Scots*, p. 208.

6. Carswell, *Brother Scots*, p. 203.

7. Carswell, *Brother Scots*, p. 209.

8. Morgan, *Keir Hardie*, p. 96.

9. Benn, *Keir Hardie*, p. 138.

10. Morgan, *Keir Hardie*, p. 99.

11. Cole, *Makers of the Labour Movement*, p. 217.

12. Maxton, Keir Hardie, p. 11.

CHAPTER 6

1. Margaret Cole, *The Story of Fabian Socialism*, London: Heinemann, 1961, p. 97.

2. Stewart, *J. Keir Hardie*, p. 158.

3. J. Keir Hardie, *From Serfdom to Socialism*, London: George Allen, 1907, p. 95.

4. Stewart, *J. Keir Hardie*, p. 178.

5. Morgan, *Keir Hardie*, p. 126.

6. Benn, *Keir Hardie*, p. 170.

7. Bob Holman, *Trading in Children. A Study of Private Fostering*, London: Routledge, Kegan & Paul, 1973, p. 264.

8. McLean, *Keir Hardie*, p. 96.

9. Morgan, *Keir Hardie*, p. 134.

10. McLean, *Keir Hardie*, p. 97.

11. Mary Hamilton, *Arthur Henderson. A Biography*, London: Heinemann, 1938, pp. 28, 53.

12. Holman, *Good Old George*, p. 48.

13. Hamilton, *Arthur Henderson,* p. 52.

14. Holman, *F. B. Meyer,* p. 96.

15. McLean, *Keir Hardie*, p. 100.

16. McLean, Keir Hardie, p. 101.

CHAPTER 7

1. Stewart, *J. Keir Hardie*, p. 251.

2. Hardie, *From Serfdom to Socialism*, p. 9.

3. Hardie, *From Serfdom to Socialism*, p. 10.

4. Hardie, *From Serfdom to Socialism*, p. 1.

5. Hardie, *From Serfdom to Socialism*, p. 2.

6. Hardie, *From Serfdom to Socialism*, p. 10.

7. Morgan, *Keir Hardie*, p. 203.

8. Smillie, *My Life for Labour*, pp. 29–30.

9. Hardie, *From Serfdom to Socialism*, p. 36.

10. Hardie, *From Serfdom to Socialism*, p. 37.

11. Hardie, *From Serfdom to Socialism*, pp. 37–38.

12. Hardie, *From Serfdom to Socialism*, p. 30.

13. McLean, *Keir Hardie*, p. 112.

14. Morgan, *Keir Hardie*, p. 156.

15. W. Knox, "The Political and Workplace Culture of the Scottish Working Class 1832–1914", in Hamish Fraser and R. Morris (eds), *People and Society in Scotland 1830–1914*, Edinburgh: John Donald, 1990, p. 159.

16. Hamilton, *Arthur Henderson*, p. 79.

17. Mary Davis, *Sylvia Pankhurst. A Life in Radical Politics*, London: Pluto Press, 1999, p. 14.

18. Benn, *Keir Hardie*, p. 232.

19. J. Keir Hardie, *India. Impressions and Suggestions*, London: ILP, 1909, p. 6.

20. Hardie, *India*, p. 90.

21. Hardie, *India*, p. 84.

22. Hardie, *India*, p. 107.

23. Hardie, *India*, p. 126.

24. Morgan, *Keir Hardie*, p. 194.

25. Morgan, *Keir Hardie*, p. 288.

CHAPTER 8

1. Benn, *Keir Hardie*, p. 264.

2. Morgan, *Keir Hardie*, p. 165.

3. Reid, "Hardie's Laurels", p. 5.

4. Benn, *Keir Hardie*, p. 287.

5. Patricia Romero, *Sylvia Pankhurst. Portrait of a Radical*, New Haven: Yale University Press, 1987, p. 34.

6. Benn, *Keir Hardie*, p. 150.

7. Benn, *Keir Hardie*, p. 113.

8. Davis, *Sylvia Pankhurst*, p. 109.

9. Morgan, *Keir Hardie*, p. 166.

10. Hughes (ed.), *Keir Hardie's Speeches and Writings*, pp. x–xi.

11. *The Guardian, First World War. The Road to War*, London: *The*

Guardian, 2008, p. 16.

12. J. Keir Hardie, *Killing No Murder! What Caused the Recent Railway Strike?*, London: ILP, 1911, p. 1.

13. Hardie, *Killing No Murder!*, p. 23.

14. Hardie, *Killing No Murder!*, p. 23.

15. Morgan, *Keir Hardie*, p. 248.

16. Stewart, *J. Keir Hardie*, p. 373.

17. Hughes (ed.), *Keir Hardie's Speeches and Writings,* pp. xiii, xv–xvi.

18. Sylvia Pankhurst, *The Home Front*, London: The Cresset Library, 1987, pp. 45, 23.

CHAPTER 9

1. Carswell, *Brother Scots*, pp. 161–64.

2. Lowe, *From Pit to Parliament,* p. 76.

3. Robert Smillie and others, *Memoir of James Keir Hardie*, London: ILP, 1915, p. 42.

4. Fenner Brockway, "James Keir Hardie (1856–1915)", in Hugh Martin (ed.), *Christian Social Reformers in the Nineteenth Century*, London: SCM Press, 1933, p. 238.

5. Brockway, "James Keir Hardie", p. 236.

6. Benn, *Keir Hardie,* p. 136.

7. Benn, *Keir Hardie,* p. 182.

8. Benn, *Keir Hardie,* p. 80.

9. Benn, *Keir Hardie,* p. 400.

10. Glasier, *Keir Hardie,* p. 65.

11. Hughes, *Keir Hardie,* p. 9.

12. Smillie, *My Life for Labour,* p. 54.

13. Hughes, *Keir Hardie,* p. 139.

14. Glasier, *Keir Hardie,* p. 5.

15. Benn, *Keir Hardie,* p. 433.

16. Stewart, *J. Keir Hardie,* p. 336.

17. Hughes, *Keir Hardie,* p. 54.

18. Hughes, *Keir Hardie,* p. 221.

19. Morgan, *Keir Hardie,* p. 287.

20. McLean, *Keir Hardie,* p. 130.

21. McLean, *Keir Hardie,* p. 130.

22. Benn, *Keir Hardie,* p. 259.

23. Holman, *F. B. Meyer,* p. 126.
24. Gordon Brown, *Maxton*, Edinburgh: Mainstream Publishing, 1986, p. 36.
25. Brockway, "James Keir Hardie", p. 235.
26. David Smith, "Evangelicals and Society", manuscript chapter, Glasgow, 2007, p. 11.
27. Smillie and others, *Memoir*, p. 7.
28. Hughes, *Keir Hardie,* p. 234.
29. Brockway, "James Keir Hardie", p. 239.

INDEX

Printed in Great Britain
by Amazon